CROSSROADS OF EMPIRE

CROSSROADS OF EMPIRE
The Europe-Caribbean
CONNECTION
1 4 9 2 - 1 9 9 2

Edited by Alan Cobley

DEPARTMENT OF HISTORY
UNIVERSITY OF THE WEST INDIES
Cave Hill   Bridgetown   Barbados

The Department of History
University of the West Indies
Cave Hill Bridgetown Barbados

CATALOGUING IN PUBLICATION DATA

Crossroads of empire; the Europe-Caribbean
connection 1492-1992 / edited by Alan Cobley.

p. cm.
Public lectures sponsored by the Depatment of
History, University of the West Indies (Cave Hill) . . .
Includes bibliographical references
ISBN 976 621 031 4
1. West Indies – History. 2. West Indies –
Civilization – European influences. 3. West Indies –
Relations – Europe. 4. Europe – Relations – West Indies.
I. Cobley, Alan. II. University of the West Indies (Cave Hill).
Department of History III. Title
F1620.3.C761994   972.9-dc-20

Typeset by Caribbean Contact Ltd
Cover design by Robert Harris
Printed by Stephenson's Lithopress Ltd

A series of public lectures sponsored by the Department of History,
University of the West Indies, Cave Hill, Barbados, the National Cultural
Foundation (Barbados) and FUJITSU-ICL Caribbean Ltd

Contents

CONTRIBUTORS

HILARY BECKLES is Reader in History and Head, Department of History, University of the West Indies, Cave Hill.

GEORGE BELLE is a Lecturer in the Department of Government and Sociology, University of the West Indies, Cave Hill.

BRIDGET BRERETON is Reader in History and Head, Department of History, University of the West Indies, St. Augustine.

SELWYN CARRINGTON is a Senior Lecturer in the Department of History, University of the West Indies, St. Augustine.

GEORGE LAMMING is an internationally renowned novelist and writer on Caribbean Affairs.

REX NETTLEFORD is Pro-Vice Chancellor, Director of the School of Continuing Studies, and head of the Trade Unions Institute at the University of the West Indies, Mona.

KATHLEEN PHILLIPS-LEWIS is a Lecturer in the Department of History, University of the West Indies, St. Augustine.

PAT THOMPSON is Chief Executive Officer of the Caribbean Association of Industry and Commerce.

KARL WATSON is a Lecturer in the Department of History, University of the West Indies, Cave Hill.

List of Abbreviations

ABC Islands	Aruba, Bonaire, Curaçao
ACP	Association of Caribbean and Pacific States
CARICOM	Caribbean Economic Community
CBI	Caribbean Basin Initiative
COMECON	Council for Mutual Economic Assistance
DOMs	Départments d'Outre-Mer
EC	European Community
GNP	Gross National Product
IMF	International Monetary Fund
NA	Netherlands Antilles
NAFTA	North American Free Trade Agreement
OAS	Organisation of American States
OECS	Organisation of Eastern Caribbean States
PRG	People's Revolutionary Government of Grenada
UK	United Kingdom of Great Britain and Ireland
UN	United Nations
UNESCO	United Nations Educational, Scientific and Cultural Organisation
USA	United States of America
USSR	Union of Soviet Socialist Republics

List of Maps

Introduction

This collection is the product of a series of public lectures delivered at the Steel Shed, Queen's Park, Bridgetown over nine weeks between February and April, 1992, under the broad title 'The Caribbean and Europe'. The lecture series, initiated by the History Department of the University of the West Indies, in association with the National Cultural Foundation, was the latest in an annual series which began in 1984. The first four series, between 1984 and 1988, marked the 150th anniversary of slave emancipation in the Commonwealth Caribbean, while the series in 1989 commemorated the 350th anniversary of Parliament in Barbados. 'The Caribbean and Europe' was the third in a series which began in 1990 with 'Africa and the Caribbean', and continued in 1991 with 'The Caribbean and the Americas'.

The History Department's annual public lecture series has become an important conduit for raising public consciousness and promoting public debate in Barbados on economic, social and cultural issues in an historical context. An integral part of each series has been the lively audience participation in question and answer sessions following each lecture, in which knowledge, ideas and experiences are shared. This participation demonstrates the insatiable thirst of the Barbadian people for a wider knowledge and a deeper understanding of the world in which we live.

In this context, the series on 'The Caribbean and Europe' was conceived in part to coincide with, and to help assess the significance of, the 500th anniversary of the European invasion of the Caribbean region which began with Columbus in 1492. 1992 is also an important watershed in Caribbean-European relationships for another reason, with the current movement in the European Community towards a single market and greater political integration. The historical position of the Caribbean region in a rapidly changing 'world order' was an important theme which emerged out of the lectures and the discussions they provoked.

This collection is intended for popular consumption, as were the lectures themselves. They are being published as far as possible as they were delivered, with some amendments to aid the transition to the written page. The most important amendment has been the inclusion of end notes in a number of cases where it was deemed necessary to identify the sources of quotations or to guide further reading. Where end notes were not deemed necessary, a list of suggestions for further reading has been added to facilitate further study on the issues raised.

This publication was made possible through the most generous financial assistance of Fujitsu-ICL Caribbean (Barbados) Limited and the Cave Hill Campus of the University of the West Indies. Special mention must also be made of Simpson Motors Limited who contributed towards the cost of staging the series. The continuing commitment shown by these corporate sponsors to support public education and development in the region is particularly heartening in these times of economic stringency. Finally, I would like to express my gratitude to the National Cultural Foundation and its staff for their help in staging the lecture series, and to the Chairpersons of each of the sessions.

Alan Cobley
University of the West Indies
Cave Hill, 1993

As a company FUJITSU-ICL Caribbean Ltd is deeply committed to communication and the dissemination of knowledge. We provide important linkages in these areas both within the Caribbean and beyond. Accordingly, it is appropriate that we should sponsor publication of this collection entitled *Crossroads of Empire: The Europe–Caribbean Connection 1492-1992*. We are also delighted to be associated with the continuing efforts of the University of the West Indies to promote a deeper understanding of and within the Caribbean region.

Ken Sylvester
Vice-President
Caribbean Manager
FUJITSU-ICL

1

The Caribbean:
Crossroads of the Americas

REX NETTLEFORD

Like the United States of America, the Caribbean in its least secure moments of half-way house existence, often describes itself in hyphenated terms. Irish-Americans, Italian-Americans, Hispanic-Americans, German-Americans and, since the 1960s, Afro/or African-Americans, have their counterparts in the archipelago of islands which stretch some four or so jet hours from the Bahamas in the North to Trinidad and Tobago in the South, with the mainland territories of Guyana on the South American Continent and Belize in Central America thrown in for good measure. The journey takes the traveller through or over the Greater Antilles, the Leeward and Windward Islands, now linked into the Organization of Eastern Caribbean States (OECS), Barbados, perching further east into the Atlantic, and Trinidad, off the coast of Venezuela. Other countries like Nicaragua, Costa Rica, Panama, Colombia and Venezuela and the Yucatan Peninsula of Mexico, all washed by the Caribbean Sea, insist that they, too, are 'Caribbean'. President Ronald Reagan attempted to seal this perception by dumping us all into what Washington since the mid-1980s has come to call the 'Caribbean Basin'.[1]

There is, then, not only the Anglophone Caribbean comprising the former and still existing colonies of Great Britain (otherwise called the Commonwealth Caribbean instead of the West Indies). There is also a Spanish-speaking Caribbean including Cuba, Santo Domingo and Puerto Rico, a Francophone-Caribbean starting with Haiti, armed with its ancestral liberation pedigree, and taking in Martinique, Guadeloupe, Guyane, St. Martin – all departments of metropolitan France, and a Dutch-speaking Caribbean covering the internally self-governing Netherlands Antilles of Curaçao, Bonaire, St. Martin, St. Eustatius and Saba as well as Aruba, and the still independent Suriname.

Speaking of tongues, the Caribbean on this basis seems a Tower of Babel. And so it is, being the crossroads of languages which are the languages of former colonisers and conquerors providing *linguae francae* for the thirty or more millions of souls who now congregate in that crossroads and are seeking to give common expression to the common soil of history and existential reality they share. Unlike the United States of America and, to some extent Canada, that underlying unity is yet to be expressed in the fact of a common polity or an accepted common cultural kernel that the federation of the United States of America and the primacy of the English language (of a particularly *American* brand) now offer the 200 million odd hyphenated inhabitants of the sub-continent headquartered in Washington.

The Caribbean has of course created many languages indigenous to the crossroads which the region has been. I refer first to the most developed of them all, *papiamento*,[2] which draws on many feeder sources to be the living tongue of the people of Curaçao who have developed enough of an orthography to have it as a scribal language of instruction in its educational system. In Suriname there is *sman tonga*[3] and in Jamaica, *Jamaica Talk* which has the distinction of creating a dictionary published by Cambridge University.[4] In Haiti, Martinique, Guadeloupe, and the former French islands of St. Lucia, Dominica and Grenada there is *patwah* (Patois) or creole;[5] and throughout there are, in addition, different levels of code-switched versions of the *linguae-francae*. None of these crossroads languages are regarded as the appropriate languages of formal discourse or official communication despite the recent declaration of creole as the official language of Haiti.[6]

A Lexicography Project has been researching the consistencies of a 'Caribbean English' which its protagonist Richard Allsopp, believes to exist in the way that American English is celebrated with all its dynamic audacity. This, I am aware, does not rule out the acknowledgement and persistence of the many regional dialects of the United States which are even now being carefully documented by none other than Frederick Cassidy, a Jamaican lexicographer who, being Caribbean by birth and upbringing, understands the crossroads dimensions of language.[7] It was he, after all, who pioneered similar documentation of Jamaica Talk. That an understanding of the sociology of language is vital to public policy and educational development in our textured hemisphere, is an imperative common to all the communities in the Americas.

There is no corresponding political centre in the Caribbean of which I speak, nor any agreed-on cultural kernel such as a common Caribbean language. Therein lies the region's strength, to be sure, but also its weakness. The plurality of forms, whatever the unanimity of feeling, is evident in other areas as well. There are religious expressions a-plenty, including orthodox Christian, orthodox Muslim, orthodox Hindu, Bahai, Pentecostal and Televangelical; but there are also crossroads syncretisms like Santeria,

Pukkumina, Voodoo, Shango, Zion revivalism, Rastafari and a variety of personal dispensations.[8] Kinship patterns range from single-parent matriarchal, through non-consanguineous extended, to nuclear family structures. The Caribbean is a region of options. Variety at the crossroads at worst spells confusion, periodically inviting self-doubt and equivocation. But at best it engenders among individuals the capacity to operate on two or more levels, sequentially or simultaneously, in dealing with the quixotic, multi-faceted social phenomena characteristic of the crossroads where disparate elements meet, contend and have their being.

As a microcosm not only of the Americas but also of Planet Earth the Caribbean is a laboratory for all the tensions (creative and disintegrative) of the human condition as we have come to know them these past 500 years and as they shall continue to show themselves in the next century.

Even in that segment of the Caribbean where English is uniformly spoken for formal discourse and the Westminster model of government inherited from Anglo-Saxon Britain forms the basis of governance, there is great variety which to some may be the spice of life but which is currently too hot for those who would wish to deepen economic integration and heighten cultural correspondences rooted in a shared history of some four centuries at least. The Caribbean Community (CARICOM) is even now servicing an 'independent West Indian Commission' set up by the thirteen Governments of this small part of the Caribbean inhabited by five million souls to formulate proposals for advancing the goals of the Treaty of Chaguaramas which, back in 1973, began the process of Caribbean integration through the Caribbean Community and a Caribbean Common Market.[9]

Santo Domingo has applied for full membership in that Community, demonstrating its own perception of its economic destiny down the decade into the 21st century. Puerto Rico has also shown interest in relating closer to CARICOM despite its own virtual integration in the mainland economy of the United States. Haiti has long regarded itself as part, if not the hub, of the Caribbean reality. And Cuba, under Castro, has for two decades described itself as a Caribbean nation on historical, cultural, economic, if not political, grounds. Yet all these countries meet at the crossroads with differing political systems and approaches to public decision-making.

Cuba's Marxism-Leninism has never really taken root in the English-speaking Caribbean with its ancestral connections to Whitehall, the two party system, parliamentary democracy and the mythology of free, fair and frequent elections. Grenada admittedly flirted with politburos and Central Committees but four years of such experimentation brought the flirtation to a suicidal end with the assassination of Maurice Bishop, the charismatic populist leader of the regime which espoused Muscovite Bolshevism but kept the Queen as its Head of State.[10] Santo Domingo and Haiti have different political systems based on the Latin inheritances of Spain and France respectively. The Netherlands Antilles still have their umbilical cords attached to Mother

Holland. Suriname, coup-ridden and beleaguered, is even now threatening to re-tie the knot,[11] to the consternation of parts in Latin America, while the Quai d'Orsay has made it abundantly clear that Martinique and Guadeloupe will retain their deputies in the French Parliament whatever may be the *Caribbean* cultural yearnings of native Martiniquans and Guadeloupians.

Such rainbow sovereignties will continue to be a serious stumbling block to any ambition for Caribbean-wide political unity. But like the wider world the crossroads mentality of the region's peoples may well lead to overlapping alliances bringing into the 21st century new forms of functional co-operation with appropriate institutional frameworks which are even now evident in other parts of the world, including the wider Americas, where a Free Trade agreement between the United States, Canada and Mexico is now on the Washington agenda.[12] In any case, the Caribbean has long known that union can be achieved other than by formal marriage. Life at the crossroads teaches pragmatism.

Geography here plays a significant role as it has played in the Single Market process of Europe but so do historico-cultural realities. The modern Americas are the result of the encounters of a number of old civilisations, starting with the Americas themselves, then Western Europe (and later Central and Eastern Europe), West Africa, the Mediterranean, and Asia. Admittedly there have emerged out of this melange of differing cultures distinctive creolised forms known severally as 'Plantation America' where Europe and Africa met and interacted on foreign soil, setting the stage for the further explorative encounters with latter day Asians (East Indians and Chinese) who came as indentured labourers, 'Meso-America' where the ancestral Native American cultures met with Europe and interacted on American soil, and 'Euro-America' where Europe overseas, despite the encounters with others, has managed to establish hegemonic political, religious, economic and social sway over large tracts of real estate and the minds of millions of souls. The segmentation is as much a function of psychological and perceptual reality as it is of the actual power and exclusive control by recognized groups of people over material and intellectual resources. But where the above cited cultural spheres co-exist in concentrated fashion, and impose on hordes of people challenges for the discovery and maintenance of new designs for social living, they constitute a kind of world that points directions for the third millenium long since indicated in the globalisation of all existence, and the contracting spheres of human activity brought in sharper focus by the immediacy of satellite communication.

The Caribbean, as crossroads, meeting place, and centre of encounters of myriad cultural elements, as well as crucible in which new forms of human expression have been forged over the past half a millenium, and are still being forged, deserves closer study and investigation by those in the Americas who are preparing the new generation for the next half a millenium.

It is in this sense that the year 1992 must be seen and not in terms of the *celebration* of a quincentennial of 'discovery' by an explorer whose accidental arrival, admittedly of great historical significance for humankind since 1492, has been distorted by the chroniclers and shapers of world history to herald, ennoble, and justify the exaggerated claims of one set of human beings in their subjugation of other sets of human beings in circumstances that cannot possibly be seen as other than oppressive by those who were involuntarily severed from ancestral hearths and made to suffer in what, to some, is still regarded as a Babylonian exile.[13] Those who were decimated by the cruelty of imported diseases and physical suffering through the exploitation of labour enough to earn the support of the Spanish cleric Las Casas,[14] are not amused by the pratings of organisers and advocates of the Quincentennial Celebrations now softened in UNESCO-ese rhetoric as the 'Encounters of the Two Worlds'.

But there is much more to such an 'encounter' as far as the Caribbean is concerned. For other encounters followed speedily enough on the so-called first encounter between Iberian Europe and Native America. There was, after all, the Middle Passage involving millions of African slaves transported to the Caribbean for sugar cultivation. And there is to this day the uneasy centrality of that phenomenon of the 'African Presence' to a region which came to mark off our part of the world from much of the rest. The 'Presence' in the crossroads has taken on important dimensions because of vigorous attempts for all of 500 years to deny it a place not only in the Americas, where Eurocentric mainstream ontologies and cosmologies still dominate all ideas for growth and development, but also in the racist Western world now grappling with the last bastion of expanionist triumphalism in the anguished struggles against *apartheid* in South Africa.

The pre-occupation with that 'Presence' in the Americas does not, however, serve to blind all those in the Caribbean to the existence of others in that crossroads, or to the inter-dependence that continues to determine the fate of all who stand (admittedly with darting eyes on all sides of their rotating heads) in that crossroads, or to the inescapable organic interactions between the occupants at the crossroads. For such interactions transform all who inhabit the space at the crossroads from being the carriers of limited dimensions of the feeder roads which brought them and their forbears, to being the current concentrated, textured and, in a sense, *different* beings we are, all with new sense and sensibility which has long made a difference to the Western world as much as the old civilisations of that world have themselves made a difference to people in the Americas. This is precisely why the White man in the Americas is as Negrified as the Black is Europeanized, with or without the loss or gain of melanin in the skin. The Caribbean, as crossroads, understands this in its daily existence despite every calculated effort from the North Atlantic to have it remain a carbon copy of that part of the triumphal West or to make it into a clone of a world which that part of the West insists it is for it, and it alone, to fashion.

It is axiomatic that out of the need to survive, the Caribbean should resist all efforts to have itself zombified, or to have its own cultural integrity negated, or to have itself deprived of its self-generating dynamic and capacity to exist beyond survival. So, despite the Tower of Babel which the tongues of different former colonial masters now make of the region, despite the mosaic of ethnic entities (including the home-grown Caribbean mixed-blood variants), despite the plurality of political systems and social orders, the various Caribbean territories find common bonds in that historical experience of resistance to slavery, colonialism and economic exploitation as well as in the aftermath of that experience indicated in racism, intellectual dependency and the on-going need for economic and cultural survival in a world that was never really organised for the sort of existence created at the Caribbean crossroads. The myth of 'Paradise' persists with a vengeance among those persons, native and foreign, who would wish to sell the region in the 'upscale market' for tourism, despite the harsh realities of an end-of-century, post-colonial world of debt, growing unemployment among the young, and social disorder consequent on poverty.[15]

The United States with the benefit of much greater material resources has admittedly done better than all others in the Americas; yet, some would insist, at a cultural price that would deny to the crossroads reality the organic presence of large segments of the United States population that now perceive themselves to be marginalised to their political, economic and cultural disadvantage.[16] And yet the Caribbean, as crossroads, shares much in common with the United States in matters of cultural assertion and the process of political self-definition vis-à-vis the claims of former masters.

It was the United States which of all territories in the Americas first won its national independence. It won it, lest we forget, by violent means, by armed resistance, a modality of liberation which was to be later taken up by Haiti and large parts of Hispanic America.[17] In the early 19th century it was the United States that was accused of exporting revolutions to Latin America while Haiti was kept constrained by the young and ambitious United States, among others, from doing the same to other slave-colonies. That little paradox of history is too often forgotten when Cuba, in its 20th century claims to sovereignty and autonomy, is made the pariah of the inter-American system by those who fail to understand the 'crossroads' imperatives of our existence in these parts.[18] Such imperatives spell liberation and self-determination, national reconstruction and, of late, the right to keep company with whomever we would wish or dare to have and hold as friends. The Anglophone Caribbean negotiated its own independence after scores of battles and skirmishes on slave plantations against exploitation, dehumanisation and oppression. But in all cases it is the collaborative efforts of all those at the crossroads who made the liberation possible – meaning Black and White, Native American and Mestizo, slave and liberal masters, Free

Coloured and White missionaries newly independent nationals and even latter day benefactors otherwise known as 'consultants'. The making of the wider Americas, like the making of the Caribbean, has been on the basis of such collaboration. Exaggerated claims by this or that category of souls in the liberation, development and modernization of the region are not likely to bring the stability of civil society which is no more guaranteed in the United States, despite its nuclear and hi-tech power, than it is in the 'developing' Caribbean, still struggling for self-possession, economic rationality and cultural certitude.

It is the absence of such certitude, interestingly enough, which makes for a certain tolerance evident at the crossroads, even if such tolerance is source of misunderstanding by those who would wish to have the entire region seek protection under their own particular umbrella. When a former President of the United States (Jimmy Carter) conceded the prudence of ideological pluralism in the hemisphere, the Caribbean offered an excellent example of what was possible. Both *between* and *within* Caribbean nations, the radicalism of the Left, so-called, survived beside both the conservatism of the Right and the middle-ground stance of large bands of what the North Atlantic would call 'centrists'. What the Oval Office subsequently discovered in Moscow that – Communist Party leaders were basically human – was something long known to Caribbean peoples who admired Fidel Castro for his courage and commitment to self-determination without wishing to adopt the political and social institutions which underpinned his revolution. Many parts of the Caribbean could admire Jeffersonian democracy without surrendering their responsibility to find their own route(s) to life, liberty and pursuit of happiness. We, in any case, also have had direct access to John Locke, but more importantly to our historical experience of denial of and threat to individual freedom, whether in slavery, indentureship, colonialism or post-colonial dependency.

The challenge is no less at the beginning of the Nineties. Despite the seeming triumph of free enterprise and *laissez-faire* economics in the world at large, some parts of the Caribbean are aware that doctrinal attachment to market forces without due consideration for the mass of disadvantaged who inhabit their shores, is a recipe for disaster. The responsibility to draw on the sensibility of crossroads reality and find the irreducible kernel of commonsense and appropriate frameworks is not lost on many Caribbean communities. We are, after all, a people of options. And nowhere is this more evident than in the English-speaking part of the region where despite the current stridency of marketforces rhetoric in some places, [19] the task of facing the infrastructural imperatives of effective primary health care, sound and accessible education and minimal durable housing for the majority had better stay on our agenda.

Despite the fullest understanding of the right to this, that, and the other which is the hallowed inheritance from the Enlightenment, freedom from hunger, from disease, from ignorance and from fear are central to the dialectic of individual liberty existing alongside social responsibility. In case we forget, it was an American President faced with the gravest problems of social and economic despair in the Depression who enunciated such freedoms as the basis for his New Deal. The Caribbean as crossroads of the contemporary Americas naturally tunes into this pattern of governance that has never failed to serve the hemisphere in time of dire need.

It is the vision of a world of phenomena, which are multi-faceted and with no claim to exclusive authorship, that has made the Americas so innovative and of such value to the rest of humankind as well as to the older worlds from which the modern Hemisphere originally sprang. We know of the products of the process of cross-fertilisation as are manifested in artistic culture, for example. No music has been composed in the world at large since the second decade of the 20th century without due reference to jazz, the great invention of the crossroads world of the United States. Other forms of music, from the Cuban 'son' of the late nineteenth century through Trinidadian calypso at mid-century to Jamaican reggae at end of century have influenced music the world over. Dance, painting, sculpture, and the graphic art of American advertising have all guided developments worldwide; while United States science and technology, from the earthly automobile to spaceships, have conspired to make a difference to the lifestyle of the global village that Planet Earth has become.

The Caribbean has produced less of such monumental material edifices but it has created innate structures of civilised social interaction in 'crossroads' communities of differing races, cultures and worldviews. These have offered models for civilised living in a world that still sets large store by prescriptive status based on ethnic origin and indefensibly exclusive claims to 'high culture'. It is the pluralist dimensions of Caribbean reality and the corresponding perceptions of life and living that remain among the greatest of the region's attributes.

For the Caribbean has learnt and still lives by the adage that 'in the house of human history there are many mansions'. It is a sophisticated view described by the great 20th century historian of ideas, Isaiah Berlin, as holding that

> there are many objective ends, ultimate values, some incompatible with others, pursued by different societies at different times, or by different groups in the same society, by entire classes or churches or races, or by the particular individuals within them, any one of which may find itself subject to conflicting claims of uncombinable, yet equally ultimate and objective ends.[20]

To the one-dimensional mind that spells schizophrenia. To the Caribbean person living in his/her historical and existential crossroads of existence, it is source for creative action; for within the expected limits of humanity, the variety of ends for human development can indeed be extensive. It is such understanding which creates among a people a genuine curiosity about other cultures and a willingness to acknowledge the inner logic and integrity of other peoples' ontologies and cosmologies. For did not the African suffer enslavement and continuing denigration 'for not having had any culture', according to his masters? And what of those would-be biologically or culturally spawned offspring of different races residing with full flush of intellectual capability in the very Caribbean?

This is an excellent point of departure for the preparation of our young for the 21st century. And yet this is nothing new, for a 19th century liberal English political philosopher, John Stuart Mill, was constrained to write the following:

> It is hardly possible to overrate the value, in the present low state of human improvement, *of placing human beings in contact with persons dissimilar to themselves and with the modes of thought and action unlike those with which they are familiar.* Such communication has always been, and is peculiarly in the present age, one of the primary sources of progress (my emphasis).[21]

If this was true of John Stuart Mill's time, how much more of ours! The Caribbean, like all the rest of the Americas, was a place where persons 'dissimilar to each other' were indeed put in contact with each other; and after four or so centuries of complex and contradictory encounters they have come up with the germ of a civilisation that has nowhere been sufficiently plumbed as a basis for educating the next generation of Americans who shall have to face similar encounters due to the contraction of the world they will inhabit. Whether the Caribbean person will take a hold of his history and have it inform his contemporary and future life is hard to say. For into the crossroads another feeder road – this time from the galactic spheres via satellite – is showering the crossroads with would-be manna from above; and many are finding the new penetration irresistibly overpowering.

For this very reason the education of the Caribbean/American child in certain directions is now vital – firstly, away from the old bigotry of a certain prejudice which attributes to members of other civilisations and other cultures, or races a self-worth less than his own because they are different; secondly, away from a bald and humourless scientism which deprives human beings of their sense of purpose and makes them into statistical units in the production process or mere anthropological specimens; and thirdly, away from a blind skepticism that gives no meaning or existence to things beyond the ken of one's own culture narrowly perceived. The task is greater than we imagine since a half a millenium of miseducation in some of these particulars will be difficult to obliterate in one fell swoop. But there can be a beginning, and the mounting of the International Social Studies conference in Miami in June, 1991 on 'The Caribbean Cradle, Crossroads and Crucible of the

Americas' can be seen as a conscious contribution to the process of safe entry into the 21st century which will demand of the Americas precisely what our origins and development over the past half a millenium have more than equipped us for, *viz* the betterment of human life. That political and other leaders through hubris, the thirst for power, and a corrupted perception of human existence have diverted American sense, sensibility and vision from the responsibilities that inhere in such an inheritance can only be laid to human failing. To err, then, is human, and to forgive divine. Without ever attempting to play God we may well forgive ourselves so that knowledge can indeed advance and human action improve. The Caribbean, precisely because it has lacked power and is itself still on the threshold of 'becoming', may well have some useful lessons to teach in this respect. For to know the Caribbean is to know much that is actually lurking in the final decade of the second millenium, of the formative second-half of that millenium and the threshold of the third millenium.

The 21st century promises either to be chaotic, or irritatingly confused and contradictory, since more than ever it will signify the crossroads of humanity, crossing, criss-crossing and producing what we in Jamaica refer to as 'crosses', meaning trouble, crisis and challenges. That process, which assumes no simple journey to truth, to liberty or to proverbial bliss is by no means alien to Caribbean experience. For the contemporary region is the continuation of a historical process rooted in the occurrences of cross-fertilising human contact this past half a millenium when a feisty sailor described by Derek Walcott as the 'Genoan Wanderer'[22] came upon lands he thought were west of elsewhere to which he had set sail by routes yet unknown to him and his kind (though already known, according to another tradition of scholarship, to West Africans and to Norsemen otherwise known as Vikings).[23]

Important, then, though 1992 must be to Iberians and all other Europeans whose history since the Middle Ages signifies a triumphalist spirit based on conquest and the expropriation of large tracts of real estate in the Western Hemisphere of which the Caribbean is a seminal and significant part, the quincentennial observance duly set for 'celebration' means something quite different to millions of 'Americans', starting with Native Americans, small branches of which continue to survive in the insular Caribbean as Caribs, though the majority of their ancestral kin died out early in the encounters with Europe's marauding hordes.[24]

Others who came to replace them, followed by others like the Asians who came later to replace the replacements, now dominate the physical and psychic spaces of the region.[25] But they, like the Europeans who came either as masters or as settlers, have undergone serious seachange, are the products of that awesome complex process of 'becoming' — creolisation and indigenisation to some, cross-fertilisation to others. They are people of a New World indeed, not the 'newness' of the historical tradition that dared to ignore the fact that the people who discovered Columbus on their beaches had been living for eons before he arrived. But 'new' they certainly are in the unprecedented sense and sensibility they carry, honed out of half a millenium of myriad encounters between old civilisations transplanted to foreign soil on the one hand and old civilisations *in situ* on the other, in circumstances that ranged from oppressive dehumanisation, resistance and wanton exploitation, through accommodation and adjustment, to genuine innovation and creativity.

It is the strengthening of that tradition of innovation and creativity demanded by the cultural and survival imperatives of the crossroads which hold out the greatest promise for the Caribbean in its quest for self-development. It holds out no less for the rest of the Americas whose contribution to humankind in the 21st century must be the enhancement of self-worth in an improved and protected natural environment, rather than the expense of invaluable thought and energy on war and the rumours of war.[26] It is, indeed, a betrayal of the American inheritance to do otherwise. The real discovery at this stage, then, is not so much that of Columbus as it is of the half a millenium sojourn by our multi-sourced millions at the crossroads. That sojourn has made possible remarkable discoveries about human possibilities, and the wide range of such possibilities, discoveries about the diversity of human endeavours and the unity that can underpin such diversity; discoveries of both the inevitability or change and the regulative principles that underly all change. What remarkable gifts we all have with which to enter the 21st century!

NOTES/SUGGESTIONS FOR FURTHER READING

1. 'President Reagan's Address to the OAS on February 24, 1982', *Bulletin* (US Department of State), March 1982. The Caribbean Basin Initiative (CBI) was a proposed plan of trade and investment incentives designed to 'improve the economic well-being of the Caribbean area' and enacted into a law known as the Caribbean Basin Economic Recovery Act (CBERA). See Carmen Deere et al, *In the Shadows of the Sun: Caribbean Development Alternatives and US Policy* (Westview Press, Boulder, 1990), Chapter 6.

2. Douglas Taylor, *Language of the West Indies* (Johns Hopkins University Press, Baltimore, 1977), also John Holm *Pidgins and Creoles*, Reference Survey, Volume II, (Cambridge Language Surveys, Cambridge University Press, 1989), pp. 312–316.

3. Joy Gleason Carew, 'Language and Survival: will Sranan Tonga, Suriname's Lingua Franca become the official language?', in *Caribbean Quarterly* Volume 28, No. 4, December 1982, pp. 1–16; also Joseph Ginnes (ed.), *Languages of the Guianas,* (University of Oklahoma, Summer Institute of Linguistics, No. 35, 1972); W.L. Hellinga, *Language*

Problems in Suriname. Dutch as the Language of the Schools,
(Bureau of Amsterdam, North Holland Publishing Company, 1955);
John Holm, *op.cit.,* pp. 433–444; J. Voorhoeve and A. Kramp, 'Syntactic Developments in Sranan', paper presented to the Society for
Caribbean Linguistics, Suriname 1982.
4. Cassidy F.G., *Jamaica Talk,* (Macmillan, London, for Institute of
Jamaica, 1961); Cassidy, F.G. LePage, R.B., *Dictionary of Jamaican
English* (Cambridge University Press, 1967).
5. Edith Efron, 'French and Creole Patois in Haiti', *Caribbean Quarterly*
Volume 3, No. 4, August 1954, pp. 199–213; also Claire LeFebvre,
H. Magloire Holly, Nanie Piou, *Syntaxe de l'Haitian* (Ann Arbor, 1982).
See John Holm, *op.cit.,* Chapter 9, especially pp. 382–7.
6. Creole was made the official language of Haiti with the new post-
Duvalier constitution of 1987. For a general discussion on Caribbean
languages see Mervyn C. Alleyne and Beverly Hall-Alleyne, 'Language
Maintenance and Language Death in the Caribbean', in *Caribbean
Quarterly* Volume 28, No. 4, December 1982, pp. 52–49; Also Mervyn
C. Alleyne, *Comparative Afro-American: An Historical-comparative
study of some Afro-American dialects* in the New World (Ann Arbor,
Karma, 1980).
7. Cassidy, F.G., *Dictionary of American Regional English, Volume 1,*
(Belknap, Harvard University Press, New York, 1985).
8. See *Caribbean Quarterly,* Volume 37, No.1, March 1991 on the theme
'The Social Teaching of the Church in the Caribbean' with Jean
Bertrand Aristide, Barry Chevannes, Peter Espeut, Michael Campbell-
Johnson, Allan Kirton, Sr. Mary Bernadette Little, Trevor Munroe,
Garnet Roper, Burchell Taylor and Ronald Thwaites as contributors.
For a good summary of Afro-American religious expressions see George
Eaton Simpson, *Black Religions in the New World* (Columbia University Press, New York, 1977).
9. See *Progress Report of the Work of the Independent West Indian Commission - Towards a Vision of the Future* (WIC, Barbados, June 1991).
10. Fitzroy Ambursley et al, *Grenada, Whose Freedom?* (Latin America
Bureau, London, 1984); also *Soviety/Cuban Strategy in the Third World
After Grenada Toward Promotion of Future Grenada* (conference
Report August 15–18, 1984) Woodrow Wilson International Centre for
Scholars, Washington, D.C.
11. Among the contending Parties in the May 1991 elections in Suriname
was 'the new Front for Democracy, a coalition of parties representing
East Indians, Creoles and Indonesians in this multi-ethnic republic on
South America's northeast coast'. The new Front for Democracy 'also
appealed for a mandate to negotiate closer links with the Netherlands'.
But it was the newly formed political movement called the Democratic
Alternative which campaigned for a 'commonwealth association with

the Netherlands': *Jamaica Record,* Saturday, May 25, 1991, p. 6.

12. The US/Canada/Mexico initiative (NAFTA) gained currency in 1991 under President Bush who also proposed the Enterprise of the Americas Initiative (EAI) for the Caribbean Basin as a companion piece.

13. The Rastafarians of Jamaica see themselves as 'exiled Africans' or Black Israelites' in Babylonian captivity (slavery followed by Western colonialism). See M.G. Smith et al, *The Rastafari Movement in Kingston, Jamaica* (ISER, UWI, Mona, Kingston, 1960); see also *Caribbean Quarterly* Volume 26, No. 4, December 1980 on the theme of 'Rastafari'.

14. The reference is to Bartolome de Las Casas, the Dominican missionary whose *Brief Relation of the Destruction of the Indies* 'is a horrifying catalogue of atrocities perpetrated during his time in Hispaniola. Las Casas devoted the rest of his long life to the cause of Indian liberty, continually urging the Crown, in his sermons and writings and by personal agitation at Court, to enact more humane legislation and to let audiencias enforce it...'. See J.H. Parry, Philip Sherlock, Anthony Maingot, *A Short History of the West Indies* 4th Edition (Macmillan London, 1987), pp. 23–24.

15. See Judith Weddeburn (ed.), *Rethinking Development* (Consortium Graduate School, UWI 1991), especially 'Rethinking Development: Out Loud' by Norman Girvan, and 'Some Reflections on Economic Development in Jamaica' by Michael Witter; also *Caribbean Studies,* Volume 24, Nos. 1–2, January–June 1991, Special Issue on Caribbean Economy.

16. The reference is to the growing concerns among Minorities in the United States about their marginalisation in a society which still functions on the basis of a White 'mainstream' culture. See Thomas Byrne Edsall & Mary D. Edsall's 'Race' in *Atlantic Monthly,* May 1991 for a 1990s view on the issue.

17. See Carolyn Fick, *The Making of Haiti: The Saint Dominigue Revolution from Below* (University of Tennessee Press, Chattanouga, 1990); also C.L.R. James, *The Black Jacobins: Toussaint L'Ouverture and the San Domingo Revolution* 3rd ed. (London, 1980).

18. Cuba is still seen as an exporter of revolutions by forces in Washington despite declarations to the contrary by Fidel Castro. The trade embargo imposed in 1961 was still in force 30 years later and the demand by Washington for democracy via elections and multi-party politics persists. Castro is adamant in the view that he must find his own path to national reconstruction and decolonisation as an alternative to being a client state of the United States, which Cuba had been from 1891 to the time of the Revolution.

19. The PNP government of Jamaica (1989–) has been frequently cited by journalist as being the clearest Commonwealth Caribbean example of the rejection of socialist policies for the free enterprise system in continuation of the initiatives of the JLP government of 1980–89 which

allied with the Republican Administration of Ronald Reagan to move the region to the Right.

20. Isaiah Berlin, *The Crooked Timber of Humanity–Chapters in the History of Ideas,* Henry Hardy (ed.) (John Murr Publishers, London, 1990), pp. 79–80.

21. *Ibid* p. 90: Berlin adds: 'This amounts to a thesis, particularly if for "progress" we substitute "knowledge", with which some critics of the thinkers of the Enlightenment (as perhaps a good many of us today) might not disagree.' This quotation and the one noted at 21 above are from the essay 'Alleged Relativism in Eighteenth-Century European Thought', in which he discusses the ideas of Vico and Herder.

22. Walcott, Derek, *Omeros,* (Farrar, Straus, New York, 1990), the stanza reads '... A Genoan wanderer saying the beds of sticks/named the place/for a blinded saint'.

23. See Ivan van Sertima, *They Came Before Columbus,* (Random House, New York, 1976); also Brigitta Wallace, 'Some Points of Controversy' in Gordon Ashe (ed.), *The Quest for America* (Praeger Publishers, New York, 1971), pp. 155–174. van Sertima's thesis is not universally accepted in scholarly circles.

24. See E.P. Banks, 'A Carib Village in Dominica' in *Social and Economic Studies,* Volume 2, 1956.

25. Asians (East Indians and Chinese) were recruited as indentured labourers after Emancipation (1938) to replace the African slaves who had replaced Arawaks and Caribs as labour in the 16th and 17th Century. Today over 50% of the population of Guyana and some 40% of the population of Trinidad are of East Indian ancestry. See David Dabydeen and Brinsley Samaroo (eds.), *India in the Caribbean* (University of Warwick, Hansib, 1987).

26. The United States as a 20th century Superpower has been cast in the role of aggressor since the end of World War II even when seen as safe-guarding world-wide democracy as in Vietnam, Grenada and the much publicised and 'celebrated' Persian Gulf War against Saddam Hussein's Iraq.

2

The Caribbean Before
and After Columbus

KARL WATSON

And all this happened to us.
We saw it,
We marveled at it.
With this sad and mournful destiny
We saw ourselves afflicted.
On the roads lie broken arrows,
Our hair is in disarray.
Without roofs are the houses,
And red are their walls with blood.

The vision of the conquered – Aztecan poem written shortly after Cortez captured the city of Tenochtitlan, capital of the Aztecan confederation.

COLUMBUS THE MAN

Much, both positive and negative, has been said and written about Columbus – there is no need here to enter the controversies generated – we are looking at the effects of his voyages rather than the specific details which would require a separate lecture – I would like however, to indicate the following.

He himself, contrary to recent assertions, was a man of the sea, with first hand experience of the West African coast down to Elmina (in present day Ghana), the Atlantic islands – Madeira, Canary Islands, Cape Verde Islands and North-Western Europe (including England, Ireland and possibly Iceland).

He most definitely did not believe that the earth was flat – most informed people of the time would have agreed that it was feasible to reach Asia by sea, but were daunted by the idea of distance. A body of cartographic and nautical information had been steadily building up in the fifteenth century based primarily on Portuguese initiatives in exploration and their utilization of local knowledge from African and Arab sources, such as Toscanelli's letter of 1474 hypothesizing the possibility of reaching the East by sailing West from Europe. Columbus did not fear the distance, because in his calculations, he consistently underestimated the earth's circumference by some 25 per cent.

In his mind, his proposal was feasible and his many rebuffs did not discourage him: 'I plough ahead no matter how the winds might lash me.' This reflects the character of the man – stubbornness and determination – he was in many respects, a visionary and it was that vision and imagination which helped to carry him and his crew across the Atlantic. Behind that drive lay two propelling forces — both equally urgent – the need to find treasure (the economic), manifested by fables of the lands of Ophir, and the urge to see Christianity triumphant, manifested in a burning desire to see Jerusalem retaken from Islam. From today's perspective, the second aim may seem overstated, but empathizing with Columbus and the extant world view, it was a perfectly understandable and desirable objective. In the Iberian Peninsula, the Cross had just defeated the Crescent, the Spanish Christian 'Reconquista' had achieved its goal of the expulsion of Islam from Europe – the year was 1492 – a door had closed, but as the *Nina, Pinta* and the *Santa Maria* slipped from the docks of Palos bound for open water, another closed door awaited its opening – the biological barrier of the Atlantic stood waiting to be breached. This would forever change the course of world history.

THE CARIBBEAN BEFORE COLUMBUS

I have thrown out the idea of the Atlantic as a barrier. This was so despite tenuous penetrations, some of which have been hypothesized and some proven. Ivan van Sertima in *They Came Before Columbus* argues strongly for a pre-Columbian contact from West Africa, citing for example the physical features of heads of the Olmec culture of Mexico. In Chile there is tantalizing archaeological evidence (Chinese ceramics) of a possible contact from China. Thor Heyerdahl has postulated a Polynesian connection. Archaeological investigations have proven the existence of Norse settlements dating from approximately A.D. 1000 in Newfoundland and evidence has surfaced to indicate that English fishermen were exploiting the Grand Banks some 20 years before 1492. Yet all these contacts were short-lived and left no imprints or alterations to the physical and cultural landscapes of the time.

During the last major glaciation, the Wisconsin glaciation, (which ended approximately 10,000 years ago) lower ocean levels permitted the appearance of a land bridge between Asia/Siberia and America/Alaska, across what is now the Bering Straits. It was across this land bridge that early man moved around 15,000 years ago (although dates as early as 20,000 B.C. have been postulated), this movement culminating an earlier long-lasting migration from man's point of origin – the Rift Valley of East Africa. He moved swiftly – radiocarbon dates of 13,000 B.C. have been established for Brazil. When man reached the islands of the Caribbean is unknown, but an estimate of 5,000 B.C. is acceptable. We have confirmation via Carbon 14 dating for the Levisa site in Eastern Cuba of 3,500 B.C. and 2,500 B.C. for the Pedernales site in the Dominican Republic. What is apparent is that the date is pushed back with new discoveries and the existence of an early pre ceramic archaic culture (true Neolithic/Stone Age) is hypothesized. We have an example of a flaked stone tool from Hellshire, Jamaica, which is tantalizingly reminiscent of the Folsom points of North America (Aarons) and early cultural indicators from St. Kitts. (Armstrong)

With the rising ocean, all biological life in this hemisphere became isolated and over time developed specific characteristics. For example, the 'O' blood characteristic is widespread among Amerindian populations. More importantly, a wide variety of species endemic to each hemisphere developed through the evolutionary process. With contact, the biological barrier was broken, with a subsequent massive, ongoing exchange of species and genes between the Old World and the New – an exchange of tremendous economic, social, cultural and biological consequences.

Fig. I: Biological balance sheet of the Columbian Exchange
(Major crops only):

From the New World	Old World
Maize	Rice
Potatoes	Wheat
Sweet potatoes/Yams	Barley
Cassava	Oats
Cotton	Sugarcane
Tobacco	

In the Caribbean, almost 60 per cent of existing plant life has been introduced. We accept much that we see around us as part of the natural landscape. The trees and shrubs are familiar to us, and seem to have always been here. But this is not the case, as any cursory listing of our plants would demonstrate. It is no exaggeration to say that the Amerindians and Columbus would be astonished at the transformation which has taken place since 1492. Large scale deforestation has taken place, native species have become extinct and imported decorative ornamentals, new types of shade trees and many new varieties of ubiquitous weeds now dot the land.

The relationship between sugar cane and corn is instructive in terms of its consequences. When corn was taken to West Africa it sparked a population explosion that fueled the traffic in humans from there to the Americas, in response to the labour demands of sugar. This altered the demographic picture in the tropical regions of the Americas, making blacks a majority in most of the Caribbean islands and creating a new socio-cultural matrix made up of West African and West European cultural forms.

In the Caribbean only a few animals were present before the arrival of

Columbus, such as hutia, the opposum, small dog, the turkey, and Muscovy duck. The introduction of horses, cows, pigs, sheep, and rats helped to change the landscape, created new economies, altered man's lifestyle and changed the course of history. For example, horse breeding was undertaken by the Spanish on their *hatos* in Jamaica, from whence Pizzaro obtained mounts which facilitated the invasion of Peru.

POLITICAL AND CULTURAL CHARACTERISTICS OF PRE-COLUMBIAN PEOPLES

There is some confusion in the naming of the various culture groups which inhabited the Caribbean islands. The Greater Antilles were populated by an Arawakan speaking people – hence known as Arawaks, but also referred to as the Taino. There is evidence of an earlier less culturally developed people, identified as the Ciboney. The Lesser Antilles were first populated by Arawaks and by a subsequent group of people known as the Caribs – this sequence and names are entrenched in the literature. Yet the people known as Caribs did not use that name themselves. They called themselves the Kalinago.

It was on Columbus' first voyage that an Indian informant on a beach in Hispaniola told the Admiral of small islands to the south occupied by Caniba (which in Taino means 'manioc people') – this to Spanish ears sounded like Caribe and so a new people was born. Caribe became the root word of both Caribbean and cannibal and to compound the error, Caribe also became synonymous with 'fierce' and 'voracious'. In Venezuela, the local word for the piranha is – Caribe. However, recent thinking (Aerie Boomert, Berund Hoff among others) suggests that the Caribs were not a distinct linguistic group, but were of Arawak descent and the myth of their fierceness was overplayed to justify Spanish slave raiding expeditions to the Eastern Caribbean. The Spanish used the concept of pagan versus infidel, and emphasized the horrors of cannibalism to justify their raids against these so called warlike Indians. In reality these peoples were conducting an understandable resistance to Spanish encroachment – but their bad reputation started in 1492 when Columbus was told that the Caniba had 'but one eye and the faces of dogs'.

The islands of the Greater Antilles (Cuba, Hispaniola, Puerto Rico and Jamaica), possessed an elite social structure based on the chief or *cacique* who headed a large extended family and maintained ties to other elite groups through marriage. He maintained his position through successful war leadership, invariably owned a large sea going canoe, manifested an ability to establish contact with supernatural forces and also manifested an ability to travel in spirit or animal form and visit supernatural/sacred areas above or below the earth. These political/religious developments reached their peak in Hispaniola. This can be attributed to the size and large population of that island relative to the others.

In the Lesser Antilles no such complex, elitist political structure was manifested among the Kalinago/Island Carib, but the political/cosmological elements found in the Greater Antilles were repeated in simpler form. There is evidence of *caciques*. Ethnographic evidence for the 17th and early 18th Centuries confirms this. The terminology of Kings is used for the leaders of Dominica, St. Lucia and St. Vincent. They maintained frequent contact with each other, communicating through the use of canoes, in an unsuccessful attempt to play off the French against the English, maintain their autonomy and in the case of St. Vincent, protect their fellow Kalinago from the growing might of the Black Caribs. Successful leadership among the Kalinago was based on:- 1) heading a large family with many sons-in-law; 2) War leadership; and 3) Canoe ownership.

In terms of culture, the Amerindians of the Caribbean were a Stone age people, but their ceramics were highly developed, and one can see marvellous examples of their work in museums in Santo Domingo, Martinique, St. Vincent and here in Barbados at our museum. There is some evidence of metallurgy as evidenced by the use of placer gold for pectorals and other body ornaments.

Housing was communal, consisting primarily of long houses, conical structures, built around a plaza, which was used for community purposes. In the Greater Antilles this included a ball plaza for the team game called *batey*. Subsistence agriculture was practiced, of the slash and burn variety, concentrating on the cultivation of cassava/yucca, corn, and tubers. This provided carbohydrates. Protein came largely from shellfish, fish and birds. Fishing was highly developed, both on reefs and in deep water, where the archaeological record for Barbados certainly shows that flying fish were caught and eaten.

Contrary to the views of Spanish chroniclers and French priests (for example, Labat, who had a Breton concept of religion), the Amerindians did have a religious system, which manifested itself in the use of sacred *zemis*. They lacked writing, their only documentary statement being their petroglyphs and pictographs, of which there are outstanding examples in Hispaniola, Jamaica, Guadeloupe, St. Vincent and Grenada. But these certainly prove their conceptualization of a supernatural world peopled by spirits and god figures with whom the shamans and *caciques* communed for the benefit and well being of the entire population.

I personally incline to Sapper's estimate of a higher population – Rosenblat's figures are far too low. All the contemporary estimates (admittedly exaggerated) point to high figures and the archaeological evidence tends to support a higher estimate rather than a lower estimate.

There has been considerable dispute over the Las Casas figure of 1,100,000 Indians for Hispaniola in 1496 (a figure he derived from Columbus). This figure was used by the demographers Borah and Cook to arrive at an estimate of 7,000,000 for the whole Caribbean in the year 1492. Rosenblat has

Fig. II: Demographic estimates of pre-Colombian populations,
showing Wide variations:

	High	Low
Hispaniola	7,000,000	100,000
Cuba	1,700,000	60,000
Jamaica	300,000	40,000
Puerto Rico	1,000,000	70,000
Lesser Antilles	300,000	150,000
Total	9,300,000	420,000

General Estimates for total Caribbean

Kroeber	Rosenblat	Steward	Sapper	Dobyn
200,000	300,000	220,000	3/4,000,000	550,000

dismissed the Las Casas figure, stating that there were no means of taking a census in 1496 and hence this was an imaginary figure concocted by Columbus to impress the Spanish sovereigns with the magnitude of his finds in the Caribbean – a high figure that was subsequently conveniently utilized by Las Casas to exaggerate the population collapse in the Indies, and at the same time, boost his image as Protector of the Indians.

But are we right in discounting contemporary eyewitness evidence? Even if we agree that there was an absence of methodical census takers, what do we make of other contemporary accounts for much smaller islands which are easier to substantiate and which all indicate the presence of large populations? Take for example, the island of Saona (today uninhabited) lying off the south east corner of Hispaniola. This was granted to Michele Cuneo (a friend of Columbus) in 1494, who proceeded to do a population count, which showed that this small island had 37 fair sized villages and an estimated population of 30,000. Extrapolating from this and similar examples, shifts the weight to an acceptance of higher estimates. We may look at the example of the Eastern Caribbean. Ripley Bullen using his knowledge of Amerindian sites for Barbados, estimated a pre contact population of 10,000. However, we may safely double this figure given the most recent evidence emerging from archaeological excavations on the island and the growing number of occupied sites. The Grenadines provides us with another example of the extensive use made by Amerindians of all available settlement opportunities; islands/islets that are today unoccupied provide extensive material evidence of human occupation from the tenth to the seventeenth centuries.

DEMOGRAPHIC CONSEQUENCES OF 1492

The native populations of these islands have disappeared except for remnant groups. Why? A multi-causal answer must suffice, including psychological trauma, ill use, overwork, disturbed social and cultural patterns, the effects of warfare and death by disease.

Dobyn declares, 'The invasion of New World populations by Old World pathogens constituted one of the world's greatest biological cataclysms.' The Major Killers were smallpox, measles, whooping cough, chicken pox, bubonic plague, typhus, malaria, diphtheria, amoebic dysentery, influenza:- various cyclical epidemics devastated the American populations, whose lack of immunities made death certain. In addition, many viral diseases were already present in the Americas prior to 1492, among them infectious hepatitis, encephalitis and polio. Other serious diseases included syphilis, Chagas disease and perhaps yellow fever, though there is some dispute as to whether this is of Old World origin.

The high levels of mortality appalled the Spaniards who were helpless to do anything about it, given the primitive level of medical knowledge existing at the time. Man's knowledge of bacteria and viruses was centuries distant, and in the sixteenth century, the notion existed that the principle cause of disease was disturbed relationships between the body's humours. This view dominated medical thinking, and bleeding whether by scalpel or leech, to restore the balance of body fluids, was favourite resort of the medical practitioner, more often than not, hastening the demise of the patient.

Las Casas' articulation of the Amerindians plight gave birth to the so-called 'Black Legend' by which the atrocities, ill-treatment and hard work exacted by the Spaniards, have been blamed as the principle factor for the disappearance of native peoples from the region. These were important and did take place. Although somewhat exaggerated in De Bry's imaginative pictorial renderings of Spanish activities in the New World, they are fully documented in official correspondence from the Indies to the Spanish Crown and by observers, especially priests. However, the charge of deliberate genocide levelled against the Spanish cannot be substantiated. For all their acts of cruelty, the Spaniards were not fools. They needed labour and were unwilling to do manual work for themselves if they could coerce others to do it for them. Thus making use of pre-existing cultural practices of the Amerindians, who used communal labour for major projects, the Spaniards attempted some continuity here. Their plan however, had one fatal flaw. It was totally opposed to the Indian world view, who gave of their labour cheerfully and willingly when it went to the glory of their gods and their *caciques* and not personal enrichment.

The Spanish materialistic world view, which stressed the individual and created wealth for selfish personal reasons was anathema to the Indians. So, very quickly, labour that was once given willingly had to be extracted through the use of brute force. Their spirit broken, their social systems collapsed and confronted by the spectre of the sword and disease, it is no wonder that the Indians largely disappeared from the Caribbean, less than a hundred years after the conquest initiated by Columbus' voyage of 1492. The sad remnant groups in Dominica and St. Vincent are a pale reflection of what once was - not a perfect world, but their world.

You tell me than that I must perish
like the flowers that I cherish.
Nothing remaining of my name,
Nothing remembered of my fame?
But the gardens I planted still are young
the songs I sang will still be sung!

(Huexotzin, Prince of Texcoco)

SUGGESTIONS FOR FURTHER READING

Crosby, Alfred W., *Ecological Imperialism. The biological expansion of Europe, 900–1900* (Cambridge University Press, Cambridge, 1986).

Cummins, John, *The Voyage of Christopher Columbus. Columbus' own journal of discovery newly restored and translated* (Weidenfeld and Nicolson, London, 1992).

Heyerdahl, Thor, *Early Man and the Ocean* (Allen and Unwin, London, 1978).

Van Sertima, Ivan, *They Came Before Columbus* (Random House, New York, 1976).

Steward, Julian, *Handbook of South American Indians* (Cooper Square Pub., N.Y., 1963).

Denevan, W.M. (ed.), *The Native Population of the Americas in 1492* (University of Wisconsin Press, Madison, 1976).

3

Kalinago (Carib) Resistance to
European Colonisation of the Caribbean

HILARY McD. BECKLES

The resistance of native Caribbean people to the colonial dispensation established by Europeans following the Columbus landfall of 1492 has received insufficient attention from scholars. Unlike the case with the experience of enslaved African people few studies have presented systematic accounts of their anti-colonial and anti-slavery struggle. The reasons for this historiographic imbalance are not altogether clear. No one has suggested, for example, that their fight for liberty, life and land was any less endemic or virulent than that of Africans. On the contrary, most accounts of European settlement have indicated in a general sort of way their determination and tenacity in confronting the new order in spite of their relative technological limitations with respect to warfare.[1]

This study seeks to specify some of the political and military responses of the Kalinago people (known in the colonial documentation as Caribs) to the European invasion as they sought to maintain control over lands and lives in the islands of the Lesser Antilles. The examination makes reference to the immediate post-Columbian decades, and touches briefly upon the early eighteenth century of the Treaty of Utrecht in 1713, but is concerned principally with the period 1624 to 1700 when Kalinagos were confronted by considerable military pressures from English and French colonising agents. During this period Kalinagos in the Windward and Leeward Islands launched a protracted war of resistance to colonialisation and slavery. They held out against the English and French until the mid-1790's, protecting some territory, maintaining their social freedom, and determining the economic and political history of the region in very important ways.[2]

According to recent archaeological evidence, the Kalinago were the last migrant group to settle in the Caribbean prior to the arrival of the Europeans in 1492. The Columbus mission found three native groups, of different derivation and cultural attainments, but all of whom entered the Caribbean from the region of South America known as the Guianas. These were the Ciboney, the Taino (Arawaks) and the Kalinago. The Ciboney had arrived about 300 B.C., followed by the Taino, their ethnic relatives, about 500 years later and who by 650 A.D. had migrated northwards through the islands establishing large communities in the Greater Antilles. Starting their migration into the islands from about 1000 A.D., Kalinagos were still arriving at the time of the Columbus landfall. They were also in the process of establishing control over territory and communities occupied by Tainos in the Lesser Antilles, and parts of the Greater Antilles. When the Spanish arrived in the northern Caribbean, therefore, they found the Tainos to some extent already on the defensive, but later encountered Kalinagos whom they described as more prepared for aggression.[3]

Kalinagos, like their Taino cousins and predecessors, had been inhabiting the islands long enough to perceive them as part of their natural, ancestral, survival environment. As a result, noted G.K. Lewis, they prepared themselves to defend their homeland in a spirit of defiant 'patriotism', having wished that the 'Europeans had never set foot in their country.'[4] From the outset, however, European colonial forces were technologically more prepared for a violent struggle for space since in real terms, the Columbus mission represented in addition to the maritime courage and determination of Europe, the mobilisation of large-scale finance capital, and of science and technology for imperialist military ends. This process was also buttressed by the frenzied search for identity and global ranking by Europeans through the conquest and cultural negation of other races.

In the Greater Antilles, Tainos offered a spirited but largely ineffective military resistance to the Spanish even though on occasion they were supported by the Kalinago. This was particularly clear in the early sixteenth century in the case of the struggle for Puerto Rico in which Kalinagos from neighbouring St. Croix came to Taino assistance. In 1494, Columbus led an armed party of 400 men into the interior of Hispaniola in search of food, gold, and slaves to which Taino *caciques* mobilised their armies for resistance. Guacanagari, a leading *cacique*, who had tried previously to negotiate an accommodating settlement with military commander Alonso de Ojeba, marched unsuccessfully in 1494 with a few thousand men upon the Spanish. In 1503, another forty *caciques* were captured at Hispaniola and burnt alive by Governor Ovando's troops; Anacaona, the principal *cacique* was hung publicly in Santo Domingo. In Puerto Rico, the Spanish settlement party, led by Ponce de Leon, was attacked frequently by Taino warriors; many Spanish settlers were killed but Tainos and Kalinagos were defeated and crushed in the counter assault. In 1511, resistance in Cuba, led by *cacique* Hatuey, was put down; he was captured and burnt alive; another rising in 1529 was also crushed. In these struggles, Taino fatalities were high. Thousands were killed in battle and publicly executed for the purpose of breaking the spirit of collective resistance; some rebels fled to the mountains and forests where they established maroon settlements that continued intermittently the war against the Spanish.[5] By the middle of the sixteenth century, however, Taino and

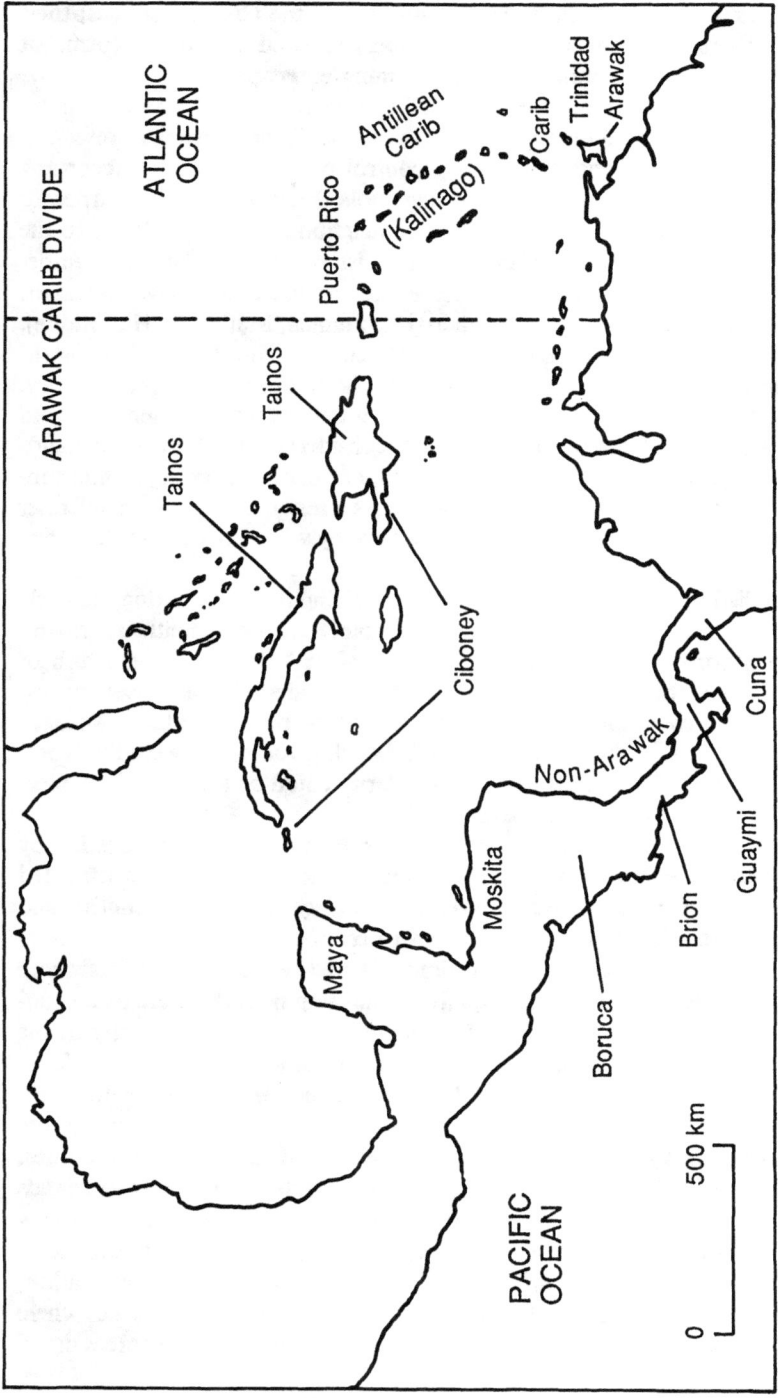

DISTRIBUTION OF ARAWAKS AND CARIBS IN THE CARIBBEAN

Kalinago resistance had been effectively crushed in the Greater Antilles; their community structures smashed, and members reduced to various forms of enslavement in Spanish agricultural and mining enterprises.

In the Lesser Antilles, however, the Kalinago were more successful in defying first the Spanish, and then later the English and French, thereby preserving their political freedom and maintaining control of their territory. According to Carl Sauer, 'As the labor supply on Espanola declines, attention turned to the southern islands' which from St. Croix, neighbouring Puerto Rico, to the Guianas were inhabited by the Kalinagos. Spanish royal edicts dated November 7, 1508 and July 3, 1512, authorised settlers to capture and enslave Kalinagos on 'the island of Los Barbudos [Barbados], Dominica, Matinino [Martinique], Santa Lucia, San Vincente, La Asuncion [Grenada], and Tavaco [Tobago],' because of their 'resistance to Christians.'[6] By the end of the sixteenth century, however, the Spanish had decided, having accepted as fact the absence of gold in the Lesser Antilles, and the inevitability of considerable fatalities at the hands of Kalinago warriors, that it was wiser to adopt a 'hands off policy' while concentrating their efforts in the Greater Antilles. As a result, the Greater and Lesser Antilles became politically separated at this time by what Troy Floyd described as a 'poison arrow curtain.'[7]

The English and French initiating their colonizing missions during the early seventeenth century, therefore, had a clear choice. They could either confront the Spanish north of the 'poison arrow curtain' or Kalinago forces south of it. Either way, they expected to encounter considerable organised armed resistance. They chose the latter, partly because of the perception that Kalinagos were the weaker, but also because of the belief that Kalinagos were the 'common enemy' of all Europeans and that solidarity could be achieved for collective military operations against them.

Having secured some respite from the pressures of Spanish colonisation by the end of the sixteenth century, then, Kalinagos were immediately confronted by the more economically aggressive and militarily determined English and French colonists. Once again, they began to reorganise their communities in preparation for counter strategies. This time, it would be a clear case of resistance on the retreat. By the 1630s, their rapidly diminishing numbers were being consolidated around a smaller group of specially chosen islands – mostly in the Windwards but also in the Leewards. By this time, for instance, Barbados, identified in a Spanish document of 1511 as an island densely populated with Kalinagos, no longer had a native presence. Europeans understood the significance of this reorganisation and resettlement of Kalinago communities, and established their infant colonies in peripheral parts of the Leeward Islands where their presence was less formidable, and in Barbados where it was now absent. The English and French, then, were aware that most of their settlements would have to come to terms with Kalinago resistance. This expectation, however, did not deter them, and they continued to seek out island niches where an effective foothold could be gained until such time as Kalinago forces could be subdued and destroyed by their respective imperial forces.

The English and French sought the passification of the Kalinago for two distinct, but related reasons, and over time adopted different strategies and methods but maintained the ideological position that they should be enslaved, driven out, or exterminated. First, lands occupied by the Kalinago were required for large scale commodity production within the expansive, capitalist, North Atlantic agrarian complex. The effective integration of the Caribbean into this mercantile and productive system required the appropriation of land through the agency of the plantation enterprise. Finance capital, then sought to revolutionize the market value of Kalinago lands by making them available to European commercial interests. By resisting land confiscation Kalinagos were therefore confronting the full ideological and economic force of Atlantic capitalism. Second, European economic activities in the Caribbean were based upon the enslavement of Indigenes and imported Africans. The principal role and relation assigned to these and other non-Europeans within the colonial formation was that of servitude. Europeans in the Lesser Antilles, however, were not successful in reducing an economic number of Kalinago to chattel slavery, or other forms of servitude. Unlike the Taino, their labour could not be effectively commodified, simply because their communities proved impossible to subdue. It was not that the Kalinago were more militant than the Taino. Rather, it was because the nomadic nature of their small communities, and their emphasis upon territorial acquisition, in part a response to the geographical features of the Lesser Antilles, enabled them to make more effective use of the environment in a 'strike and sail' resistance strategy. Kalinago, then, while not prepared to surrender either land or labour to Europeans, were better placed to implement effective counter-aggression.

Primarily because of their irrepressible war of resistance, which intimidated all Europeans in the region, Kalinago were targeted first for an ideological campaign in which they were established within the European mind, not as 'noble savages,' as was the case with the less effective Taino, but as 'vicious cannibals' worthy of extermination within the context of genocidal military expeditions. Voluminous details were prepared by Spanish and later English and French colonial chroniclers on the political and ideological mentality of the Kalinago, most of whom called for 'holy wars' against 'les sauvages' as a principal way to achieve their subjugation.

This literature, dating back to Columbus in 1494, in a contradictory fashion, denied Kalinago humanity while at the same time outlined their general anti-colonial and anti-slavery consciousness and attitudes. In the writings of Jean-Baptiste du Tertre, Sieur de la Borde, and Pere Labat, for example, all late seventeenth century French reporters of Kalinago ontology, they are presented as a people who could 'prefer to die of hunger than live as a slave.'[8] Labat, who commented most on their psychological profile, found them to be 'careless and lazy creatures,' not at all suited mentally to arduous, sustained labour. In additon, he considered then a 'proud and indomitable' and 'exceedingly vindictive' people who 'one has to be very careful not to offend,' hence the popular French Caribbean proverb, 'fight a Carib and you must kill him or be killed.'9

The French discovered, like the Spanish before them, noted Labat, that it was always best, if possible, 'to have nothing to do with the Kalinago.' But this was not possible. Relations had to be established, and here Europeans discovered, Labat noted, that the Kalinago knew 'how to look after their own interests very well.' 'There are no people in the world,' he stated, 'so jealous of their liberty, or who resent more the smallest check to their freedom.' Altogether, Kalinago world view was anathema to Europeans, thus the general view, echoed by Labat, that 'no European nation has been able to live in the same island with them without being compelled to destroy them, and drive them out.'10

The English and French started out simultaneously in 1624 with the establishment of agricultural settlements in St. Kitts. From there, the English moved on to Barbados in 1627, and between 1632 and 1635 to Antigua, Montserrat and Nevis, while the French concentrated their efforts during the 1630s at Martinique and Guadeloupe. The first three years at St. Kitts were difficult for both English and French settlers. They were harassed and attacked by Kalinago soldiers, and in 1635 the French at Guadeloupe were engulfed in a protracted battle. French success in their war with Kalinago at Guadeloupe encouraged them during the remainder of the decade to expand their colonial missions, but failed to gain effective control of the Kalinago inhabited islands of Grenada, Marie Galante, and Le Desirada. Meanwhile, a small English expedition from St. Kitts to St. Lucia in the Windwards, the heart of Kalinago territory, was easily repelled in 1639. The following year Kalinagos launched a full-scale attack upon English settlements at Antigua, killing fifty settlers, capturing the Governor's wife and children, and destroying crops and houses.11

While English settlements in the Leewards struggled to make progress against Kalinago resistance, Barbados alone of the Windwards, forged ahead uninterrupted. Unlike their Leewards counterparts, early Barbadian planters rapidly expanded their production base, made a living from the exports of tobacco, indigo and cotton, and feared only their indentured servants and few African slaves. By 1650, following the successful cultivation of sugar cane with African slaves, the island was considered by mercantile economic theorists as the richest agricultural colony in the hemisphere.

St. Kitts colonists, both English and French, determined to keep up with their Barbadian competitors, were first to adopt a common military front with respect to Kalinago resistance. During the 1630s they entered into agreements, in spite of their rival claims to exclusive ownership of the island, to combine forces against Kalinago communities. On the first occasion, they 'pooled their talents,' and in a 'sneak night attack' killed over eighty Kalinagos and drove many off the island. After celebrating the success of their military alliance, the French and English continued their rivalry over the island until 1713 when the matter was settled in favour of the English by the Treaty of Utrecht.

The success of Kalinagos in holding on to a significant portion of the Windwards, and their weakening of planting settlements in the Leewards, fueled the determination of the English and French to destroy them. By the mid-seventeenth century, European merchants, planters and colonial officials, were in agreement that Kalinagos 'were a barbarous and cruel set of savages beyond reason or persuasion and must therefore be eliminated.' By this time it was also clear that the slave-based plantation system, demanded an absolute monopoly of the Caribbean, and tolerated no 'alternative system'.[12] What Richard Dunn referred to as 'Carib independence and self-reliance' constituted a major contradiction to the internal logic of capitalist accumulation within the plantation economy.[13] As a result, therefore, the economic leaders and political representatives of this increasingly powerful production and trade complex were determined to bring the contradiction to a speedy resolution by any means necessary or possible.

By the mid-seventeenth century, the need for a full scale war against the Kalinagos, though clearly established and articulated in Spanish colonial thinking during the sixteenth century, now assumed greater urgency with the English and French. By this time, the English were first to successfully establish productive structures based on sugar cultivation and black slavery, and not surprisingly took the lead in attempting the removal of principal obstacles to the smooth and profitable expansion of the system. Also, the English with the largest number of enslaved Africans in the region, were concerned that efficient control on their plantations would be adversely affected by the persistence of Kalinago resistance.

It did not take long for the Africans to become aware of Kalinago struggle against Europeans, and to realise that they could possibly secure their freedom by fleeing to their territory. Labat, who studied inter-island slave marronage in the Lesser Antilles during this period, stated that slaves knew that St. Vincent was easily reached from Barbados, and many escaped there 'from their masters in canoes and rafts.' During the formative stage of this development, between 1645 and 1660, the Kalinago generally took 'the runaway slaves back to their masters, or sold them to the French and Spanish,' but as the Kalinago came under intensive attack during the mid-century, Labat noted, their policy towards African maroons changed. They refused to return the Africans, he stated, and began regarding them 'as an addition to their nation.' By 1670, Labat estimated that over 500 Barbadian runaways were living in St. Vincent. This community was reinforced in 1675 when a slave ship carrying hundreds of Africans to Jamaica via Barbados ran aground off the coast of Bequia. Survivors came ashore at St. Vincent and were integrated in the maroon communities. By 1700, Labat stated, Africans outnumbered Kalinagos at St. Vincent.[14] In 1675, William Stapleton, Governor of the Leewards, noting the significant presence of Africans among the Kalinagos suggested that of the 1,500 native 'bowmen' in the Leewards six hundred of them 'are negroes, some runaway from Barbados and elsewhere.'

Throughout the second half of the seventeenth century Europeans tried unsuccessfully to exploit the sometimes strained relations between Kalinagos and Africans by encouraging the former to return runaways to their owners. Miscegenation between the predominantly male African maroon community and Kalinago females was a principal cause of social tension between the two ethnic groups.[15] Both the French and English alleged that Kalinago leaders occasionally sought their assitance in ridding their communities of Africans. The significance of such allegations, however, should be assessed against the background of two important developments in African-Kalinago relations. First, by the mid-seventeenth century, the group of mixed bloods, now known as the Garifuna, was increasing rapidly in numbers, and by 1700 had outnumbered both parent groups in St. Vincent.[16] Second, joint African-Kalinago military expeditions against the French and English were common, and represented a principal characteristic feature of anti-European activity — on both land and sea. The full scale attack on the French at Martinique during the mid-1650s, for example, involved both African and Kalinago forces. The warriors who attacked French settlements at Grenada during the same period and kept them in a weak and defensive condition were also described as having an African component. Similarly, noted Labat, the English expeditions from Barbados sent to capture St. Vincent during the 1670s were repelled by both Africans and Kalinagos.[17]

The presence of effective anti-colonial Kalinago communities on the outskirts of the slave plantations, therefore, constituted a major problem for slave owners in so far as they fostered and encouraged African anti-slavery. The merging of Kalinago anti-colonial and African anti-slavery struggles, therefore, represented the twin forces that threatened the very survival of the colonising mission in the Windwards. As such, Europeans with the greatest economic stake in the enterprise of the Indies wasted no time in adopting a range of measures to suppress the Kalinago. Both the English and French pursued an initial policy characterised by the projection of anti-Kalinago social images in Europe, while seeking at the same time to promote diplomatic efforts to settle territorial claims.

In 1664 a Barbados document entitled 'The State of the Case Concerning our Title to St. Lucia,' described the island as being 'infected' with Kalinagos who were 'abetted by the French' in their war against English settlers. In this document, Barbadians sought to reject French claims to the island by stating that they had purchased it from du Parquet, the Governor of Martinique, who had bought it from the Kalinagos in 1650 for 41,500 livres.[18] Likewise, in 1668, Thomas Modyford, Governor of Jamaica, former Barbados Governor and sugar magnate, described St. Vincent, another Kalinago stronghold in the Windwards, as a place which 'the Indians much infect.' These statements represent part of the ideological preparation of the English mind for what would a genocidal offensive against the Kalinago that London merchant houses were eager to finance.

But a full-scale war, the English and French knew, would be costly, both in terms of human life and capital, and they hoped it could be averted. The significance of an ultimate military solution was clearly perceived by Kalinago leaders and colonial officials alike. The Kalinago, by participating in tactful diplomatic intrigue designed to exploit differences and conflicts between Europeans, sought to advance their own interests. In 1655, for example, Captain Gregory Butler informed Oliver Cromwell, the Protector, that the settlement at Antigua was unable to get off to a good start on account of frequent molestations by the Kalinagos, who at that time seemed to be in league with the French.[19] Again, in 1667, Major John Scott, an imperial Commander-in-Chief, reported that he led an expedition against Dutch settlements in Tobago with the 'assistance of a party of Caribs.' During the second Dutch war, 1665–1667, in which France and Holland allied against the English in the Caribbean, the Kalinago played an important role in shifting the balance of power between Europeans while at the same time seeking to expand the scope and effectiveness of their own war of resistance.[20] In June 1667, Henry Willoughby stationed in the Leewards informed his father William Lord Willoughby, Governor of Barbados, that when he arrived at St. Kitts he received 'intelligence' of further atrocities committed by the Kalinagos against the English which were 'instigated' by the French. European rivalry, Michael Craton concluded, was effectively used by the Kalinago nation, as evident in the delayed loss of St. Lucia and Grenada, and in the longer retention of full control over St. Vincent and Dominica.[21]

The English and French also targeted the Kalinago for diplomatic offensives. The first systematically pursued diplomatic effort by the English to establish a footing within Kalinago territory in the Windwards was the Willoughby initiative of 1667. William Lord Willoughby, Governor of Barbados, had long recognised the great financial gain that would accrue to himself, Barbados, and England, if the Windwards, the last island frontier, could be converted into slave-based sugar plantations. For over a decade, the sugar kings of Barbados had been signalling their demand for lands on which to expand their operations, and the Windwards were the perfect place given prevailing economic concepts about the conditionalities of slave-based sugar cultivation. Small scale military expeditions had been repelled by the Kalinago since the 1630s, and so Willoughby, not yet organised for a large scale military assault, opted to send emissaries to open negotiations with Kalinago leaders.

The Kalinagos, in response, showed some degree of flexibility, as is often the case with peoples involved in protracted struggles. Willoughby wanted a peace treaty that would promote English interests by removing obstacles to slave plantation expanionism, but the Kalinago were suspicious and vigilant. In 1666, they were tricked by the English to sign away by treaty their 'rights' to inhabit Tortola, and were driven off the island. The Windward Islands were their last refuge, and their seige mentality was now more developed than ever.

On March 23, 1667, Kalinago leaders of St. Vincent, Dominica and St. Lucia met with Willoughby's delegation in order to negotiate the peace. At the signing of the Treaty were Anniwatta, the Grand Babba, (or chief of all Kalinagos), Chiefs Wappya, Nay, Le Suroe, Rebura and Aloons. The conditions of the treaty were everything the Barbadian slavers wanted at that particular stage of developments:

1. The Caribs of St. Vincent shall ever acknowledge themselves subjects of the King of England, and be friends to all in amity with the English, and enemies to their enemies.
2. The Caribs shall have liberty to come to and depart from, at pleasure, any English islands and receive their protection therein, and the English shall enjoy the same in St. Vincent and St. Lucia.
3. His Majesty's subjects taken by the French and Indians and remaining among the Indians, shall be immediately delivered up, as also any Indian captives among the English when demanded.
4. Negroes formerly run away from Barbados shall be delivered to His Excellency; and such as shall hereafter be fugitives from any any English island shall be secured and delivered by as soon as required.[22]

The Willoughby initiative was designed to pave the way for English colonisation of the Windwards, using Barbados as the springboard for settlement. In essence, it was an elaboration of a similar agreement that was made between the defeated Kalinago and victorious French forces at Martinique after the war of 1654-1656. On that occasion, noted Jean-Baptiste du Tertre, who described in detail the nature of the conflict and its resolution, the French were able to obtain settlement rights from the Kalinago, as well as guarantees that they would assist in the control of rebel slaves by not encouraging, and more importantly, returning all runaways.[23] Within two months of the Kalinago-Willoughby Treaty, a party of fifty-four English colonists from Barbados arrived at St. Vincent in order to pioneer a settlement. The Kalinago, Garifuna, and Africans objected to their presence, drove them off the island, and broke the Treaty with Barbados.

The collapse of the Barbados diplomatic mission angered Governor Willoughby who swiftly moved to the next stage of his plan – a full scale military offensive. His opportunity came in March the following year when English military commander, Sir John Harman, left behind in Barbados a regiment of foot and five frigates. Willoughby informed the Colonial Office that since he knew not how to 'keep the soldiers quiet and without pay' the only course open to him was to 'try his fortune among the Caribs at St. Vincent'.[24] Once again, the Kalinago proved too much for Willoughby, and the expedition returned to Barbados having suffered heavy losses.

English awareness of Kalinago solidarity and efficient communications throughout the islands of the Lesser Antilles meant that they had reasons to expect reprisals for the Willoughby offensives anywhere and at anytime. Governor Modyford of Jamaica, a most knowledgeable man about Eastern Caribbean affairs, had opposed Willoughby's war plan. He told the Duke of

Albemarle that while Willoughby was 'making war with the Caribs of St Vincent' he feared the consequences for settlers at Antigua, and other places. Such an untimely war, he said, 'may again put those plantations in hazard, or at best into near broils.' 'It had been far better,' he continued, 'to have made peace with them, for if they assist the French against us,' the result would be 'the total ruin of all the English islands' and a 'waste of the revenue of Barbados.'

Modyford was perceptive in his assessment of Kalinago responses. A report sent to the Colonial Office in London from officials in Nevis dated April 1669, entitled 'An Intelligence of an Indian Design upon the People of Antigua,' stated that 'The Caribbee Indians have lately broken the peace made with Lord Willoughby, and have killed two and left dead two more of His Majesty's subjects in Antigua.' Reference was made to twenty-eight Kalinago warriors who arrived from Montserrat in two canoes and who participated in the raid upon Antigua in response to Willoughby's war in St. Vincent.

In addition, Governor Stapleton of the Leewards, in a separate document, outlined his fear for the lives of Leeward Islanders, including those who had gone to work in a silver mine in Dominica under an agreement with the Kalinago. The Barbadians also offered their criticisms of Willougby's war effort. In 1676, Governor Atkins described it as a 'fruitless design,' whose overall result was that there remained 'no likelihood of any plantations upon Dominica, St. Vincent, St. Lucia and Tobago.' Meanwhile, the Antiguans were forced to keep 'fourteen files of men...doubled three days before and after a full moon' as a protective measure against Kalinago warriors.

Governor Stapleton, reflecting on the collapse of the Willoughby initiative, and considering the prospects for English settlements in the Leewards and Windwards, quickly moved to the frontstage what had been Willoughby's hidden agenda. The destruction of "all the Caribbee Indians' he concluded, could be the 'best piece of service for the settlement of these parts.' In December, 1675, a petition of 'Several Merchants of London' addressed to the Lords of Trade and Plantations in support of Governor Stapleton's extermination thesis, called for the granting of a commission to Philip Warner, Stapleton's deputy, to raise soldiers to go into Dominica to 'destroy the barbarous savages.'

Stapleton, however, had pre-empted the Colonial Office in their response to the London merchants and had already sent Warner 'with six small companies of foot,' totalling 300 men, into Dominica for revenge on the 'heathens for their bloody perfidious villanies.' One William Hamlyn who participated in the Warner expedition, described the assault upon the Kalinago as a massacre. At least thirty Kalinago, he said, were taken and killed on the first round, not including 'three that were drawn by a flag of truce' and shot. After these executions, Hamlyn reported, another 'sixty or seventy men, women and children' were invited to Warner's camp to settle matters over entertainment. These were given rum to drink and when Warner 'gave the signal,' the English 'fell upon them and destroyed them.' Included in those killed by the English was Indian Warner, Philip Warner's own half-brother, whose mother was a Kalinago, and who had risen to become a powerful Kalinago leader. Warner was imprisoned in the Tower, tried for the murder of his brother, but was found not guilty. The decision pleased the London merchants who described him as 'a man of great loyalty' whose service to the Crown in the destruction of the Kalinagos 'who have often attempted to ruin the plantations' should be commended.

In spite of losses sustained in Dominica, Kalinagos there continued to use the island as a military base for expeditions against the English. In July 1681, 300 Kalinagos from St. Vincent and Dominica in six *periagos,* led by one who named himself Captain Peter, and who was described as a 'good speaker of English having lived for some time in Barbados,' attacked the unguarded English Settlements in Barbuda. The English were caught by surprise. Eight of them were killed, and their houses destroyed. The action was described as swift and without warning.

Frustrated again by his inability to protect the lives and property of Leeward Islanders, Stapleton reiterated his call for a war of extermination against the Kalinagos. He wrote to the Colonial Office:

> 'I beg your pardon if I am tedious, but I beg you to represent the King the necessity for destroying these Carib Indians...We are now as much on our guard as if we had a christian enemy, neither can any such surprise us but these cannibals who never come *'marte aperto'*...'[24]

If their destruction cannot be 'total', insisted Stapleton, at least we must 'drive them to the main.' He was aware, however, of the inability of Leeward Islanders to finance a major war effort, and had also become respectful of Kalinagos' ability to obtain intelligence with respect to their plans. Given these two circumstances, Stapleton instructed London to order the Barbados Government to prepare the grand design against the Kalinagos. Barbados, he added, was closer to the Kalinago 'infested' islands of St. Vincent and Dominica; also, on account of the colony's wealth, it would be the 'best piece of service' they could offer England whilst there was 'amity with the French.'

Colonial officials in London accepted Stapleton's plan in its entirety. They instructed him to make plans to 'utterly suppress' the Kalinagos or 'drive them to the main.' They also directed Governor Dutton of Barbados to make all possible contributions to the war effort. Dutton, however, would have no part of it, but not wishing to contradict the King's orders; he informed the Colonial Office that though he was in agreement, Barbadians would support no such design against the Kalinagos for three reasons. First, they consider the affairs of the Leeward Islands none of their business. Second, they do not consider the advancement of the Leewards as a good thing, indeed they considered it in their interest if the Leewards would decline rather than progress. Third, planters considered peace with the Kalinagos in the Windwards a better objective as this would assist them in securing cutwood and other building materials from those islands.

The Leeward Islanders, therefore, had to look to their own resources to finance their military operations. In June 1682, a bill was proposed to the Leewards Assembly requesting funds to outfit an expedition against the Kalinagos in Dominica. The Council agreed, but the Assembly of Nevis dissented on the grounds that since they had not been attacked by the Kalinagos in over twenty years they did not intend to endanger their peace. Months went by and Stapleton failed to get his planters to agree on a financial plan for the expedition. By 1700, the grand design had not yet materialised.

When on the 11th April, 1713, England and France settled their 'American' difference with the Treaty of Utrecht, Kalinago were still holding on tenaciously to considerable territory. St. Vincent and Dominica, though inhabited by some Europeans, were still under their control, and they were fighting a rear guard war to retain some space at St. Lucia, Tobago and Grenada. Since the French feared that successful English settlement of Dominica would lead to the cutting of communications between Martinique and Guadeloupe in times of war, they continued to assist the Kalinagos with information and occasionally with weapons in their anti-English resistance. The best the English could do was to continue the attempt to settle private treaties with the French, as they had done during the Peace of Ryswick in 1697, which enabled them to go unmolested to Dominica for the sole purpose of purchasing lumber from the Kalinago.

Kalinagos, then, succeeded in preserving some of their territorial sovereignty and by so doing were able to maintain their freedom from European enslavement. While other native Caribbean peoples suffered large scale slavery at the hands of Europeans, the Kalinago were never found in large numbers working the mines, latifundia, or plantations in the Lesser Antilles. Though Spanish slave raids during the sixteenth century did take many into the Greater Antilles to supplement Taino labour gangs, European controlled productive structures in the Lesser Antilles were not built and maintained on the basis of a Kalinago labour supply.

The involvement of Kalinagos into the colonial economy, then, tended to be small scale, and confined to areas such as fishing, tracking and hunting, agricultural consulting and a range of petty domestic services. When, for example, a group of Barbadian sugar planters, concerned about the shortage of white indentured servants, and the rising cost of African slaves, encouraged Captain Peter Wroth in 1673 to establish a slave trade in Kalinagos from the Guianas, colonial officials instructed Governor Atkins to make arrangements for the return of all those 'captured and enslaved.' The reason being, they stated, was that 'considering the greater importance of a fair correspondence between the Carib Indians and the English' in establishing settlements on the Amazon coast, it was necessary that 'provocation be avoided' and all proper measures be taken to gain their 'goodwill and affection.' Governor Atkins, in informing his superiors of his compliance indicated his agreement that it was necessary to 'keep amity' with Kalinago, since they have 'always been very pernicious, especially to the smaller Leeward Islands.'[25]

Between 1492 and 1700 the Kalinago population in the Lesser Antilles may have fallen by as much as 90 percent, noted Michael Craton, but they had done much to 'preserve and extend their independence.'[26] By this time the Dominica population, according to Labat, 'did not exceed 2000' and warriors were 'too weak in numbers to do any serious harm' to European colonies.[27] Nonetheless, colonists in the 'outlying districts' still had reasons to believe that any night Kalinago warriors could take them by surprise and 'cut their throats and burn their houses.'[28] By refusing to capitulate under the collective military might of the Europeans Kalinagos certainly kept the Windward Islands in a marginal relation to the slave population complex of the North Atlantic capitalist system for two hundred years, and in so doing, made a principal contribution to the Caribbean's anti-colonial and anti-slavery tradition.

NOTES/SUGGESTIONS FOR FURTHER READING*

* This discussion draws extensively on primary sources. For a more detailed version of this paper, including a full listing of primary sources, see Hilary Beckles, 'Kalinago (Carib) Resistance to European Colonisation in the Seventeenth Century' in *Caribbean Quarterly* Vol. 38, Nos 2/3, 1992.

5. On Kalinago assistance to Tainos in Puerto Rico see Carl Sauer, *The Early Spanish Main* (University of California Press, Berkeley, 1966), pp. 158–192.

6. C. Sauer, *The Early Spanish Main*, pp. 35, 180, 193; see also G. Lewis, *Main Currents*, p. 64.

7. Troy S. Floyd, *The Columbian Dynasty in the Caribbean, 1492–1526* (University of New Mexico Press, Alburquerque, 1973), p. 97.

8. See G. Lewis, *Main Currents*, p. 64; Richard Dunn, *Sugar and Slaves: The Rise of the Planter Class in the English West Indies, 1624–1713* (New York, 1973), p. 24; Sieur de la Borde, *Relacion des Caraibes* (Coleccion, Paris, 1694); Jean Baptiste Du Tertre, *Histoire Generale des Antilles Habitees par les Francais* (Paris, 1667–71); John Eaden (ed.), *The Memoirs of Pere Labat, 1693–1705* (Frank Cass, London, 1970).

9. *Memoirs of Pere Labat*, p. 75.

10. ibid., pp. 83, 98, 104, 109.

11. D. Watts, *The West Indies*, pp. 171–172; Richard Sheridan, *Sugar and Slavery: An Economic History of the British West Indies* (Caribbean Universities Press, Bridgetown, 1974), pp. 80, 85, 87, 456.

12. G. Lewis, *Main Currents*, pp. 104–105.

13. R. Dunn, *Sugar and Slaves*, p. 246.

14. *Memoirs of Pere Labat*, p. 137.

15. C. Gullick, 'Black Carib Origins and Early Society', in *Transactions of the Seventh International Congress on Pre-Columbian Cultures of the Lesser Antilles* (Quebec, 1978), pp. 283–287.

16. William Young, *An Account of the Black Charaibs in the Island of St. Vincent's* (1st Pub. 1795, Reprint London, 1971), pp. 5-8; see also Vancy Gonzalez, *Sojourners of the Caribbean: Ethnogenesis and Ethnohistory of the Garifuna* (Chicago, 1988).

17. Hilary Beckles, *Black Rebellion in Barbados: The Struggle Against Slavery, 1627-1838* (Carib Research and Publications, Bridgetown, 1988), p. 36.

18. Rev. C. Jesse, 'Barbadians buy St. Lucia from Caribs', *Journal of the Barbados Museum and Historical Society (JBMHS) Vol. 32, Feb. 1968, pp. 180-182.*

19. *Vere L. Oliver, History of the Island of Antigua* Volume I (London, 1894-1899), p. xix, xxv; see also R. Sheridan, *Sugar and Slavery*, p. 87.

20. D. Watts, *The West Indies*, pp. 242-243.

21. M. Craton, *Testing the Chains*, pp. 22-23.

22. A Copy of the Treaty between William Lord Willoughby and several of the Chief Captains of the Caribs, dated 23 March, 1668, can be found in *Calendar of State Papers, Colonial Series*, 1661-1668, No. 1498.

23. J.B. Du Tertre, *Histoire Generale*, pp. 467-468.

24. Sir William Stapleton of Lords of Trade and Plantations, 16 August, 1681, *Colonial Papers* Vol. 46, No. 45.

25. Jerome Handler, 'Amerindians and their Contribution to Barbados Life in the Seventeenth Century', *JBMHS* Vol. 35, 1971, pp. 112-117; and J. Handler, 'The Amerindian Slave Population of Barbados in the Seventeenth and early Eighteenth Centuries', *JBMHS* Vol. 33, No. 3, 1970, pp. 111-135.

26. M. Craton, *Testing the Chains*, p. 23.

27. *Memoirs of Pere Labat*, p. 115.

28. ibid., pp. 110-111.

4

The British West Indies Economy and The Industrial Capitalist Revolution 1775–1846

SELWYN CARRINGTON

It is almost impossible to investigate the contribution of slavery and the slave trade to the economic development of western societies without coming into contact with Eric Williams' *Capitalism and Slavery*. Around this book has developed a debate over the factors giving rise to the abolition of the slave trade and slavery. This argument has continued first with its republication in 1964, and then with the publication of Seymour Drescher's *Econocide: British Slavery in the Era of Abolition* in 1977.[1] It is in *Capitalism and Slavery*, that Eric Williams argues, by linking the profitability of the British slave trade and West Indian slavery with the significant growth of the British economy, that these gave rise to capital formation which in turn led to the industrialization of Britain. The work also establishes the thesis that in the recent stage of British industrial development, many industries relied almost totally on West Indian agricultural development. He also extends the thesis to establish that when the industrial system had matured significantly, even the industries which depended on the West Indies joined in the movements for the abolition of the slave trade and then slavery.

Based on the Williams position that Britain adopted and expanded the slave trade and slavery when these were profitable to the British Empire, the corollary emerged that the abolition of the slave trade, and the emancipation of the slaves occurred when the British West Indies were unprofitable, and their interests began to conflict with British economic goals. Williams thus went on to expand his argument to the logical conclusion that the movement for free trade which found its most ardent supporter in Adam Smith, whose publication *The Wealth of Nations* occurred at a time when events had converged to make the sugar islands unprofitable, had in the final analysis led to the passage of the Sugar Duties Act and the Corn Laws of 1846.

The debate over free trade and the contribution of the West Indies to British economic growth also occurred at a time when there were doubts among the planter class that the islands could continue profitable production over long periods. Furthermore, it was evident too to contemporary writers that:

> The cultivation of sugar by means of slavery was never successful in the long-race. As the system was managed in the British colonies, sugar estates could not possibly form a permanently profitable investment of capital. A system leading to the destruction of the lives of the labourers engaged in it, could not fail to be ultimately ruinous.[2]

It is clear that the free trade movement was tied to the demands of the rising finance capitalist class in Britain which felt restricted by the maintainance of British mercantilist policy. In essence there was dichotomy in the way in which mercantilism sought to restrain the colonial trade within the orbit of its merchant class, and the same time establish, without any restraint, access to a world-wide supply market whose production was expanding much faster in relation to West Indian output in both real and relative terms. Then, of course, there was West Indian demand for no competition in its home market. This, the planters believed would enable them to reduce sugar production in order to achieve prices which were cost effective. In fact, it seems to me, that these eighteenth century planters were very much capitalist in their own ways and clearly perceived one of the corner-stones of capitalist doctrine, the supply demand theory and its operation on prices.

Many of Williams' contemporaries had understood his vision of the inability of the sugar islands to rationalize their industry in order to overcome the changes which had occurred to the West Indian economy as a result of the American Revolution and British postwar policy.[3] These writers were in agreement with the contention that at the end of the eighteenth century, the sugar colonies had lost their pre-eminence in the British economic system and this had enabled the abolitionists to make headway in their fight for the ending of the slave trade.

In fact, these contemporary critics had accepted the traditional interpretation of Victorian scholars who had commented on the irony of British abolition. William Darity states clearly that the Williams decline thesis was in an 'incipient form in English economic history during the Victorian period.'[4] The most significant writers are William Cunningham, William E.H. Lecky and Samuel T. Coleridge. These writers have in their works argued that the West Indian sugar economy had demonstrated several weaknesses at the end of the eighteenth century. These were especially damaging because the British government had established restrictions which inhibited the colonies' continued growth. Cunningham highlights the struggle between the landed gentry in England and the emerging capitalist class involved in trade and manufacturing. This new group thus clamoured for access to cheaper natural resources. Hence, there emerged a struggle between the landed interests and the moneyed men over certain principles. Consequently, 'at the end of the eighteenth century British industrial development was assuming capitalist forms, and the capitalists were therefore demanding greater freedom from restriction of every kind which involved the abolition of bygone institutions.'[5] The foundation of British restrictive policy was the slave trade. The abolition of this pillar meant the initiation of the dismantling of the system.

Taking a world view of British mercantilism, these writers also demonstrated that as the American Revolution had destroyed the trade between colonial merchants and their counterparts in Spanish and Portuguese America, metropolitan merchants filled the vacuum. They established direct trade with these areas thus destroying the islands as entrepots of British re-exports to these areas. Colonial merchants were thus displaced as middlemen in the profitable free port trade. It is quite clear from the analysis adopted by Cunningham, Lecky and Coleridge that the abolition of the slave trade did not result from any humanitarian favour. Furthermore, it occurred at a time when its destruction was forecast to cause no significant loss to the British or to the West Indian planter class.

The critics agreed with Williams' claims that several economic factors had heightened the plight of the sugar planters. Probably the most damaging was the emergence of other producing areas of tropical commodities. These included territories inside and outside the British Empire, such as Mauritius, Cuba and India. They also offered better opportunities for investment of British capital, while at the same time producing cheaper sugar for the home market.

However, they were relentless in their criticism of what they called Williams' economic deterministic position – one which subordinated the role of the abolitionists in an effort to establish the primacy and pre-eminence of the economic forces. While it is true that the study down-plays the role of the humanitarians, as well as that of the slaves, Williams examines their contribution. Of the humanitarians, he states emphatically that *Capitalism and Slavery* had

> deliberately subordinated the inhumanity of the slave system and the humanitarianism which destroyed that system. To disregard it completely, however, would be to commit a grave historical error and to ignore one of the greatest propaganda movements of all time. The humanitarians were the spearhead of the onslaught which destroyed the West Indian system and freed the Negro. But their importance has been seriously misunderstood and grossly exaggerated...[6]

Unfortunately, these very critics who castigate Williams work for their vision of his omission also have refused to evaluate that part of the book which examines the contribution of the colonials, and the slaves to abolition. In the penultimate chapter of *Capitalism and Slavery*, Williams examined the role of the three colonial classes – The planters (the whites), the free people of colour, and the slaves – towards the question of slavery.

In this section, he basically suggested that slavery was doomed from all quarters – from the rise of finance capitalism, from the work of the 'Saints'/humanitarians and from the slaves who 'were not prepared to wait for freedom to come to them as a dispensation from above.' But, the role of finance capitalism was given the greatest weight.

The re-emergence of *Capitalism and Slavery* has continued the interest in the basic tenets of the study. Using modern approaches to social sciences research and economic analysis, researchers have cast doubts on the two theses which highlight the contribution of the plantation system to the formation of capital in Britain and its instrumentality in financing the Industrial Revolution. Instead, they contend that the islands were net drains on Britain. They thus site duty preferences, administrative and defence costs as being chiefly responsible for this situation. However, new research has debunked this argument. Nuela Zahedieh has argued quite convincingly that the merchants of Jamaica made handsome profits from their trade in manufactures and from the *asiento* with the Spanish colonies. They plunged these profits into agriculture and many merchants became planters.[7] Furthermore, she writes:

> Defence and administration costs incurred in the mother country were nominal. The Island did not have a standing army after the disbandment of Cromwell's troops in 1662. There were never more than two naval frigates stationed at the Island in this period. Frequently, there was none at all. The governors' expenses and salary were usually paid out of the proceeds of local taxation and prize goods. The Navigation Acts, which compelled the colonial producers to send their sugar to the mother country, rather than to the market of their choice, tended to reinforce the price fall of the 1670s and 1680s in England caused by supply outstripping demand. Thus, in this period, they operated in favour of the home consumer rather than the colonial producer.[8]

Zahedieh thus concludes emphatically that the wealth of Jamaica was created out of the profits from enterprises in Jamaica. Hence, the theory that colonies were burdens and costs to the mother country is wrong as far as Jamaica is concerned. In fact, in Zahedieh's opinion, the operation of the island's economy provides 'a good example of imperialism as theft.' Robert Carlyle Batie arrives at more or less the same conclusion, as far as Barbados is concerned. He contends that the sugar revolution was financed from the agricultural and business exploits of the colonists during the pre-sugar plantation days.[9] In fact, in the final analysis, Smith and his followers – the neo-Smithians – are wrong in their assumption that the money invested in the plantation system originated in England.

The other line of argument initiated to counter Williams' profitability thesis is that the slave trade was unprofitable and as a business activity it could not have led to high profits. William Darity Jr. and Joseph Inikori reject this argument and emphasise that 'on the average, the slave trade was relatively a high paying line of British industry.' Furthermore, in spite of the apparent decline of West Indian slavery, 'the rate of return on the British slave trade...tended to exceed the general rate of profit in British industry throughout the 18th century. Thus, it also tended to lift the general rate.'[10]

Another major criticism has come from those who contend that the British West Indies were not in decline but were prospering at the end of the eighteenth and early nineteenth century. Hence, the abolition of the slave trade was thus a measure of great humanity which affected West Indian slavery leading to its decline after 1807. This has within its conceptualization a basic contradiction. Why would a trade that was unprofitable and contributing little to British economic development cause such as economic catastrophe on its abolition? It is clear that Williams had accurately pinpointed the fundamental reasons for the abolition of the slave trade and slavery. Consequently, some metropolitan historians, in collusion with a few West Indian commentators who have not done in-depth research, are fighting a rearguard battle to re-establish among blacks the view that the freedom of their foreparents was dependent on the unceasing efforts of a group of abolitionists.

Of the historians involved in what I call the anti-decline perspective, Seymour Drescher, in *Econocide: British Slavery in the Era of Abolition*, establishes his main arguments which are closely aligned to Roger Anstey's position as delineated in *The Atlantic Slave Trade and British Abolition, 1760–1810*. The basic thesis of the anti-declinists revolves around Drescher's argument that in both absolute and relative terms, the economy of the old sugar colonies increased significantly at the end of the eighteenth century, reaching levels in excess of those before the American Revolution. Hence, in their opinion, both the slave trade and slavery were expanding, not contracting, in the period after 1783.

Having only recently carried out extensive and very detailed research in archives and repositories throughout Britain, I would like to share with you my conclusion, based on insurmountable evidence, that Drescher's analysis of the period is askew and that Williams' argument that the introduction of capitalist structures in the organization of the British economy was mainly responsible for the ending of the slave trade and slavery is very much closer to the truth in so far as historians can achieve it.

Having looked at the theoretical issues surrounding the state of the West Indian economy at the end of the eighteenth century, we must now examine the impact of the expansion of finance capitalism and the growth of industrialization on the slave trade. In order to comprehend how capitalist structures in Britain impacted on the British West Indies and restricted its advancement, we must examine in depth the end of the eighteenth century in order to understand how these affected negatively in the West Indian economy and destroyed the very system that assisted the creation and development of capitalism.

The West Indian economy made minimal profits in its trade with Britain only. It depended to a large extent on the export of minor staples to the

American colonies and later the United States. Prior to 1775, the Thirteen Continental colonies consumed the bulk of all minor products, especially rum, manufactured in the islands. Thus, the loss of the American market compounded the indebtedness of West Indian plantations.

Even before the American War of Independence, significant changes were already emerging in the structure of trade between the American and West Indian colonies in order to reflect more capitalist operations. This was primarily because of the decline of the sugar economy. One significant organizational change was the disappearance of speculative venturing and the emergence and growth of the commission business in American-West Indian commerce. As in Britain, some of the financial arrangements of the trade were based on credit. The period of payback was calculated on the perceived strength of the sugar industry in each colony. In the years before 1763, this could extend to a year, but the time was shortened to three to six months depending on how depressed was the state of the economy.

After 1783, as a result of the restrictive policy of the British government towards the American trade, credit arrangements virtually disappeared. British merchants and planters were thus forced to pay for their plantation supplies in cash which led to a drain of money from the islands. However, it was the loss of credit which deepened the economic plight of planters, and lessened the profitability of the sugar industry. The same thing was happening in England, and the sugar industry could not sustain the bills of exchange drawn on factors. Rum which was accepted as payment for American supplies was now rejected in most instances. This continued for the rest of the period.

The problem of credit also emerged in Britain's commercial relations with its West Indian colonies. This inability of the sugar market to consume West Indian sugar at the end of the eighteenth and the beginning of the nineteenth century deepened the indebtedness of the planters and forced many factors to initiate changes in their credit facilities. They abolished the practice of drawing bills on shipments of commodities, in an effort to safeguard their own credit arrangements with the banks; since the failure of the West Indian sugar economy could bankrupt many commissioned houses. One agent in writing to his sugar planter when rejecting his appeal for more credit stated:

> ...for if any unforseen circumstances at a crisis so alarming, should disappoint your Lordship with the Remittance you intend making us, as a provision for your Bills, it may prove injurious to our Credit, when every means of assisting rest entirely on the Sale of Produce, under the very irksome state in which we have already represented our Market to be, and which the most desponding imagination could not have suggested at the time we first had the Honour of being introduced to your Lordship.[11]

The failure of British merchants/factors to maintain their credit dealings with the British West Indian planters was undoubtedly because of their notion of the declining state of the islands' economies. The artificial nature of the plantation system thus became glaringly clear to investors and creditors alike who saw greater investment possibilities in newly cultivated territories whose soils were better suited to sugar production. All of this occurred at a time when the sugar producing areas such as Mauritius and the East Indies stepped up their output. Exports from other slave societies such as Puerto Rico, Cuba and Brazil were also competing successfully with British sugar in European markets. The result was declining sales of West Indian products on the London market, as well as a marked decline in the re-export trade.

This latter problem was particularly distressing to West Indian sugar producers because it led to the overstocking of warehouses and in the end to a significant decline in prices. The destruction of the Saint Domingue sugar industry as a consequence of the slave revolt there resulted initially in marked price increases for muscovado (unrefined sugar) in Britain. This situation also promised significant gains for the West Indians much to the distress of the sugar refiners. Hence, in 1792 they sent a petition to Parliament in which they blamed the sugar planters' monopoly of the British market for the decline of their own flourishing industry. Thus, they called for the admission of foreign sugar in British ships at higher duties and also for the equalization of duties on West and East Indian sugar. These demands signalled virtually the destabilization of the British West Indian sugar industry and efforts were immediately put in train to achieve this by the reduction in sugar prices.

Almost immediately, Parliamentary legislation was secured for this purpose. The excessive exportation of sugar was cutback by the adjustment of the drawback and bounties in relationship to the price and duties. In 1791, the entire duty was returned on re-exports of muscavado, but in 1796 while the duty amounted to 17s.6d per cwt., the drawback was lowered to 13s.6d. Two years later, the duty increased to 19s.4d, but the drawback was not increased. In 1799, the duty on sugar was further increased to 22s per cwt. However, the drawback fell to 11s. By 1803, the damage had been done. The London market was overstocked; supply had outstripped demand and prices plummeted. To safeguard the sugar industry, the drawback on re-exports once more equalled the duty at 24s. Similarly the bounty on refined sugar was also reduced in 1796; it declined further in 1799. Without both the drawback and bounty, British colonial sugar could not be sold on European markets at the competitive world prices.

Yet another method of destabilizing the West Indian economy was the reintroduction on the London market of East India sugar first imported in the seventeenth century. On the application of the grocers and refiners, in 1791 five tons of that commodity were brought into England at very high duty charges. This met with demands for lower rates of duty and although this was not adopted immediately, the die was cast. East India sugar imports were now brought in to offset high sugar prices at the end of the eighteenth century. Furthermore, British sugar manufacturers and grocers now eyed the cheaper Bengal sugar as replacement for the expensive West Indian sugar.

Another more devastating acknowledgement was made; India was able to provide a dramatically larger market for British manufactured goods. In addition, Indian labour was 'free', plentiful and cheap.

Not only was colonial sugar imported as a competitor to that from the West Indies, British merchants were permitted to import duty free foreign sugar and coffee for manufacture and re-export to European markets. This destabilizing policy had its effect. The West Indian sugar industry was further depressed and led to significant migrations from the Leeward Islands to Demerara, Trinidad and Puerto Rico. One estimate placed the number of proprietors who emigrated from Barbados, Grenada and St. Vincent at 500. The adverse consequences of British policy in the West Indies led to a call for a meeting of delegates from all islands to plan a common West Indian response. This never took place but it was not because there was not a common dislike for British policy. One commentator in reporting the pulse of the West Indians stressed that the planters were so enraged:

> ...that it is hard to form any opinion of what the consequences may be –
> It is sayed that Lord Hawkesbury (when Mr. Jenkinson) once Declared that
> Great Britain would do better without the sugar colonies than with them.
> The planters now assert that the measures of the present minister are so
> adverse and inimical in the islands that there cannot remain Doubt of his
> Intention to adopt Lord Hawkesbury's Opinion, and to shake them.[12]

West Indian plantation records are replete with complaints about the large quantity of raw sugar in warehouses in Britain. One factor told his absentee planter:– 'the stagnation of sales keep the warehouses full and prevents the sugar now in the River being landed...'[13] At times there was hardly any warehouse space as new sugar was landed upon old sugar. This situation is clearly demonstrated by numerous complaints of which the following is an example:

> From the best information I can obtain the sales of sugar do not amount
> as yet to one half of the import of the Leeward Islands fleet – of Jamaica
> sugar very little has yet been sold – and indeed of the Leeward Island sugar
> which now occupys the warehouses does not meet rapid sales. The loading
> of the Jamaica must be impeded.[14]

Two years later, the situation did not change and in 1801 warehouses were still full. Thus, one commentator noted that it was

> not expected that much sugar will now be sold before Xmas and that we
> shall have near 100,000 hhds remaining for the spring demand... and which,
> contemplating earlier arrivals in consequence of peace...will be more than
> sufficient to answer any demand which can be expected. The sugar from
> Demerara and Surinam have sadly interfered with those from Jamaica.[15]

The British sugar market continued in the same depressed condition throughout the first two decades of the nineteenth century. It became worse in the 1820s when the Indian sugar interest, supporting free trade and demanding greater imports of sugar with which to pay for British exports, applied for the admission of its sugar at West Indian duties. In 1825, the British government made this concession for sugar from Mauritius, but this was not enough and the sugar refiners demanded more. Thereafter, there was a gradual erosion of discriminatory duties until the passage of the Sugar Duties Act in 1847, and the abandonment of all preferences in the 1870s.

The increase in the price of sugar which occurred as a result of the slave revolt in St. Domingue did not last very long. Britain, as I have shown, adopted policies to arrest this rise and by June 1792 the price had fallen appreciably. However, they did not remain low but fluctuated throughout the 1790s until about 1799 when they fell to pre-war levels and then declined further for the rest of the period.

Did high prices bring automatic profitability to West Indian plantations? Historians who support the view that high profits were realised from the increased prices of the French Revolutionary period and the Napoleonic Wars overlook the high rate of inflation within the economy and advanced costs which the planters had to face. Isaac Dookhan draws attention to this issue when he stressed that the increased value to trade was 'due not to increased output even though the produce of the captured colonies was diverted to Britain, but rather to an increase in prices consequent upon social and economic disruption in the French colonies.'

In spite of the economic decline which was evident in an assessment of the West Indian economy at the end of the eighteenth century, the importance of the colonies to Britain did not fall-off with their declining profitability. This was because there was a significant growth in the amount of revenue which was extorted from the plantations as a result of rising duties and taxes. In fact, the islands had become the major source of revenue for the British war effort. Even though the quantity of sugar retained for home consumption grew by roughly 120 per cent, the value of revenue through duties increased by some 400 per cent between 1789 and 1814. Consequently, it could be argued irrefutably that the major beneficiary of higher earnings from sugar imports into Britain was not the planters/West Indian interest, but the British Treasury. Almost 45 per cent of the gross receipts of the sugar planters went to pay duties. Hence, because of rising expenses and increased taxes, the returns on capital invested in the British West Indies were too low to attract serious investors, as was pointed out by a sugar agent who wrote:

> ...an estate which 105 years ago did with a capital of less then £10,000 in slaves produced an average income of above £5,000 per annum does now with a capital of about 3 times that number not produce £3,000.... During this period the profits of land have been at least trebled.

> The defalcation of Colonial prosperity has been the eagerness of government to relieve all other taxation by over taxing ... the colonies ... the sugar kept them from extinction its profits were reduced exceedingly low till

St. Domingo was revolutionized & the British planter for a short time has the market of the world.[16]

That monopoly of the world was like a dream; a dream that was shattered by British policy of destabilization. The only monopoly which the West Indian planters were allowed was that of the British market until 1825 when some intra-imperial sugar was placed on equal footing. Colonial monopoly of the home market was only temporarily retained to secure the abolition of slavery, especially since the sugar refiners continued to make demands for its abolition, and were therefore allowed to import foreign sugar for refining and re-export. The refiners themselves pointed to this contradiction in British policy which barred the introduction of slave grown sugar for home consumption while allowing slave grown cotton and coffee.[17]

These commodities had been produced in the West Indies for many years and their output even increased towards the end of the eighteenth century. As a minor staple for most of the period, coffee was important to Jamaica and the Ceded Islands. Coffee from the British West Indies was never consumed at home in any large quantities, although its growth was encouraged in Jamaica after the 1770s. Most of the coffee imported into England from the sugar colonies was re-exported. The same observation is true for cocoa imports.

The cocoa industry was probably one of the most established and growing British concerns towards the end of the eighteenth century. As in the case of the sugar industry, its development was highly dependent on West Indian production. Cotton growing was thus encouraged in many of the newly settled islands, and in the older ones which had available land or in which sugar cane cultivation was severely affected by borer infestation or by other pests and blast. The British government had gone so far as to provide loyalist settlers with land, cotton seeds and information on the growing of cotton in order to safeguard a supply for the fledgling industry. The success of cotton cultivation had given rise to the invention of the first cotton gin in Barbados. It was a windmill whose inventor, Pearce Archer, claimed that it was able to gin and wind cotton. After an investigation, the Assembly of Barbados, on a private member's bill tabled by Robert Hind, voted the inventor a sum of money to encourage its development.

There was no protection for the cotton industry as there was for sugar, and its expansion was limited. However, it was the advent of the steam engine and the commercial development of Eli Whitney's cotton gin that expanded the cotton industry in the United States. This led to the significant expansion of slavery and to its entrenchment in American society. West Indian production was far too limited for British demand and therefore American cotton, although slave grown, found a ready market in Britain. Manchester which became the centre of the cotton industry also developed as one of the most hostile areas to the sugar planters' monopoly of the British market. It strongly supported the abolition of slavery.[18] In short, therefore, there was evidently a great deal of hypocrisy in the position of the British capitalists whose economic interests dictated the level of their anti-slavery stance.

Another area in which British industrial finance capital was invested was shipping, which during the heyday of the slave trade and slavery relied to a great extent on the West Indian economy. However, towards the end of the eighteenth century, it soon found the West Indian sugar monopoly of the home market irksome. Throughout most of the eighteenth century, British shipowners found adequate business in trades related almost solely to the sugar industry. The West Indian planters in justifying their demands for their continued monopoly of the home market pointed to the gains made by British shipping. Furthermore, they cited the West Indian trade as providing a nursery for the Royal Navy which gave it the supremacy of the seas.

However, the American Revolution released a potential giant in the shipping industry, one which was likely to be a major threat to Britain. It is clear almost immediately after the American War that British policy of exclusion did not restrict significantly United States shipping involved in the carrying trade to the sugar islands. The growth of United States shipping in West Indian commerce, as well as the international trade, continued in the period 1794 to 1806 for which detailed statistics are available. Added to the problem was the fact that most of the vessels were manned by American seamen.

Even the slave trade had lost its position as one with great investment potential. The number of seamen who died in the trade was significantly higher than in all other trades. For this reason alone, some contemporaries called for its abandonment. Eric Williams points out that towards the end of the eighteenth century the shipowners' interest in the slave trade had dropped off markedly. The capital invested in it fell from about 5 per cent in 1790 to roughly 1.25 per cent in 1807. In terms of actual shipping, it accounted for only 2 per cent of the tonnage and 4 per cent of the seamen employed in the British export trade. The shipping interest continuously blamed West Indian sugar monopoly for its failure to secure homeward cargoes from places such as Brazil, Indian and other foreign sugar producing countries. In order for British ships to procure full cargoes on their return voyage, the ship owners believed that the monopoly of the sugar interest had to be terminated. Hence, in order to secure this, they voted against West Indian slavery. Yet, the shipowners endeavoured to retain their own monopoly. They safeguarded their own monopoly by controlling the importation of slave grown products in British ships manned by British seamen.

The importance of the West Indies to British economic developments is well known. Richard B. Sheridan has developed the 'three-legged' theory in order to explain the props which were themselves instrumental in energizing the West Indian trade. These were the American trade, the British Isles trade and the African trade. The loss of these supports in the three decades after 1775 spelt virtual doom for the colonies. The first leg fell off as a result of the American War of Independence. The second leg was severely injured by the failure of British consumption to meet the expanded supply sent those from the islands during the French Revolutionary and early years of the Napoleonic Wars. This leg became a stump. The final leg was cast adrift with the abolition of the slave trade which removed the main source of plantation labour.[19]

How did the growth of capitalism affect the slave trade and how did it lead to abolition? Some historians led by Seymour Drescher have argued that Britain abolished the slave trade when it was most profitable, and when it was at its most 'absolute peak ... by volume and profitability'.[20] One nineteenth century writer has examined this very charge which was made by his contemporaries regarding the decline of Jamaica. In his rebuttal, he has stressed that the abolition of the slave trade or slavery 'was not needed to ruin the Jamaica sugar-planters, and that the system was doomed to destruction from inherent causes'.[21] Some modern writers have also rejected Drescher's claims, noting that the British slave trade to the West Indies peaked in the 1720s and 1730s, and again in the years shortly before the American Revolution. The annual British shipments of slaves from Africa rose from about 22,000 in the years 1749–1755 to approximately 37,200 between 1763 and 1775. David Richardson thus tells us that in the latter years, British vessels transported 'more slaves from Africa than in any previous or subsequent period of thirteen years'. Hence, the slave trade had 'reached its peak before, not after the War of American Independence'.[22]

Given the declining state of the slave trade – by number and profitability, by decreased tonnage, by employment of seamen, by the lack of investment possibilities, compounded by the extremely heavy losses of seamen by mortality, Liverpool merchants did not oppose its abolition.

Slavery as a labour system was not conducive to the growth of capitalist structures in the sugar economy. The Cubans found this out towards the end of the nineteenth century. Under this labour system, it was difficult, almost impossible, to mechanize sugar production and to separate it from the agricultural sector so that cane could be treated as a commodity. In addition, slavery consumed at an alarming rate its labour force which was not seen as being made up of human beings. The slaves were capital. Hence, every slave who died at the end of the eighteenth century sunk another nail into the system's coffin. In many cases, and in fact, throughout the British West Indies, the loss in capital on slave purchases was high, given the expanded increase in prices, amounting to approximately 71 per cent in the period 1775 to 1791. Seasoned slaves reached as high as £120 each.

Thus, as a result of the spiralling costs, planters were expending large amounts of capital which was normally drawn on their accounts in England, for purchasing a labour force which was not likely to make profits on that investment. Writing in 1788, the Reverend James Ramsay quoting Edward Long estimated that 'in all the islands the survivors of African slaves never' paid 'for the cost and expense of the whole lot.' Hence, he thus concluded that the importation of new slaves was unprofitable and only served to increase planters' debts.[23] Furthermore, estimates show that a healthy slave's life-span as a field hand was approximately seven years.[24] Only on a few estates was the number kept up by natural increase.

Given this inability of the plantation to maintain slave population levels, and therefore rejuvenate the labour force, it seems that slavery was indeed 'the dearest species of labour in the world'. Contemporary writers thus called for a withdrawal of capital investments from the slave trade on the grounds,

> that the same capital or even one half of what is so employed if invested in any species of domestic industry, would be attended with abundantly a greater mass of national prosperity – a greater public revenue, more shipping, more seamen, more wealth....[25]

Even if new research has attempted to reverse these observations, it is evident that many of the claims against the West Indies at the end of the eighteenth century were justified. The islands could not feed themselves from their internal resources. They could not produce or maintain their labour force by natural or any other increases; their capital had long ago disappeared to Britain; they could not employ the large amount of shipping they had done for most of the eighteenth century. British investors were tired of being held back by monopolies. They therefore directed their attack against West Indian slavery since the planters were so fond of contending that their rights to the monopoly stemmed from the compact which they had with English fellowmen – the West Indians maintained the slave trade by producing sugar which the British were committed to purchase, thus giving them protection in the home market. Consequently, the capitalists' attack on British slavery was really an attack on West Indian monopoly. The fact that British capital continued in the slave trade for decades after its abolition highlights the contradiction and hypocrisy of these capitalists and their supporters.[26]

It is sometimes difficult for writers to pinpoint exactly when events converged to impact upon other events or practices. It is also difficult to determine the overall importance of one as against the other. At the end of the eighteenth century, free trade philosophy had made such deep in-roads upon British thinking that the Cabinet had considered the abolition of the slave trade before the abolitionists became vocal in their demands. Slavery certainly could not exist within an advancing industrial system where mechanization and technological changes, so tied to educational advancement, were vital to the development of the productive areas in light of the fact that the raw material produced in the West Indies could be more advantageously procured from satellite economies. Self interest was fast becoming the watch-word of British policy makers, and since the government had established the right to legislate for the colonies, the decision to abolish the slave system by beginning with the slave trade was made without great feelings of humanity towards blacks or planters.

In 1788 the British government sent out an extraordinarily large and diverse list marked 'Heads of Enquiry' requesting governors to respond to the queries in order to enable Parliament to discuss the slave trade and slavery at its new session. In reminding the governor of Grenada that his replies were not yet received, Lord Sydney, Secretary of State wrote:

> It is also to be wished that the Council and Assembly (or the Committee to whom the management of the business may have been entrusted, in case the legislature should not be sitting) should without loss of time prepare the fullest instructions for their agents here, or any person whom they may think proper to authorize, so as to enable them to represent to Parliament the manner in which the Interests of the Islands may be affected, by any measures which may be proposed for abolishing or restraining the further importation of Negroes from the coast of Africa....[27]

The growth of service industries and investment capital, and the decline of profits from the slave trade had no doubt convinced Britain to withdraw its national participation. Individual merchants remained deeply involved in this critical area. By the end of the eighteenth century, the trade had served its purpose. Bonds and other interests bearing investments were doing better than either the slave trade or the West Indian sugar industry. Furthermore, the Industrial Revolution had developed a sense of a greater British role in international trade/commerce. This could be achieved by capital investments in any economy; the British West Indies had thus served their purpose. The expansion of British capitalism which occurred at a faster pace at the end of the eighteenth century called for the abolition of the slave trade and slavery in the same way that its emergence had destroyed European feudalism.

NOTES/SUGGESTIONS FOR FURTHER READING

1. Key works cited in the text include:- Eric Williams, *Capitalism and Slavery* (Deutsch, London, 1964); Seymour Drescher, *Econocide. British Slavery in the Era of Abolition* (University of Pittsburg Press, Pittsburg, 1977); Roger Anstey, *The Atlantic Slave Trade and British Abolition, 1760-1810* (Macmillan, London, 1975).
2. Hall Pringle, *The Fall of the Sugar Planters of Jamaica* (London, 1869), p. 12.
3. For an assessment of this theme see Selwyn H.H. Carrington, *The British West Indies During the American Revolution* (Foris Publications, Dordrecht and Providence, R.I., 1988); see also S. Carrington, 'The American Revolution and the British West Indian Economy', *Journal of Interdisciplinary History* Vol. XVII, No. 4, Spring 1987, pp. 823-850.
4. William Darity Jr. 'The Williams Abolition Thesis before Williams', *Slavery and Abolition* Vol. 9, No. 1, May 1988, p. 31.
5. William Cunningham. *Growth of English Industry and Commerce* (C.U.P., Cambridge, 1910).
6. Eric Williams, *Capitalism and Slavery*.

7. Nuela Zahedieh, 'The Merchants of Port Royal, Jamaica and Spanish Contraband Trade, 1655-1693', *William and Mary Quarterly* 3rd ser. Vol. 43, 1986, p. 593.

8. _____, 'Trade, Plunder and Economic Development in Early English Jamaica', *Economic History Review* 2nd ser. Vol. XXXIX, No. 2, 1986, p. 222.

9. Robert Carlyle Batie, 'Why Sugar? Economic Cycles and Changing of Staples on the English and the French Antilles, 1627-1654', *Journal of Caribbean History* Vols. 8/9, 1976.

10. William Darity Jr. and Joseph Inikori, 'Profitability Inside and Outside the Atlantic Slave Trade, the 18th Century Record' (Unpublished Paper: September, 1991), p. 29. I wish to thank Professor Darity for sending me this copy and for allowing me to quote this definite conclusion.

11. Davidson & Graham to Lord Penrhyn, 22 July 1803. Penrhyn MS. 1322.

12. Extract of letter written by Michael Keane, Attorney General (St. Vincent), 3 June, 1792. C.O. 260/11.

13. Thomas Plummer to Sir Joseph Foster Barham, 26 October, 1799. MS Clarendon dep. C. 361/2.

14. Plummer to Barham, 13 August 1799.

15. Plummer to Barham, 20 November 1801. Ms. Clarendon dep. C. 362/1.

16. Plummer to Barham, (no date). MS. Clarendon dep. C. 375.

17. Williams, *Capitalism and Slavery*, pp. 165-166.

18. ibid., p. 157.

19. See Richard B. Sheridan. 'The West India Sugar Crises and British Slave Emancipation, 1830-1833', *Journal of Economic History* Vol. 21, No. 4, 1961, p. 539.

20. Seymour Drescher, 'Econocide, Capitalism and Slavery: A Commentary', *Boletine de Estudios Latin-americanos y del Caribe* No. 4, June 1984.

21. H. Pringle, *The Fall of the Sugar Planters of Jamaica,* p. 16.

22. David Richardson, 'The Slave Trade, Sugar and British Economic Growth. 1776', *Journal of Interdisciplinary History* Vol. XXII, No. 4; see Cunningham, *The Growth of English Industry and Commerce.* 5th ed., P. 57. Cunningham endorses the claim that the slave trade had attained its peak prosperity shortly before the commencement of the American War.

23. Reverend James Ramsay, A.M, *Objections to the Abolition of the Slave Trade with Answers...* (London, 1788).

24. H. Pringle, *The Fall of the Sugar Planters of Jamaica.*

25. *Arthur Young. Annals of Agriculture and Other Useful Arts* (London, 1788), Vol. IX, pp. 92, 93, 96.

26. David Eltis. *Economic Growth and the Ending of the Atlantic Slave Trade (Oxford University Press, New York, 1987), p. 101.*

27. *Lord Sydney to Governor Edward Matthey, 6 November 1788. C.O. 101/28.*

5

Independence and the Persistence of European Colonialism in the Caribbean

BRIDGET BRERETON

Rapid decolonisation in the Caribbean – that is, the formal disengagement from empire by the European colonial powers – since World War Two has reduced the remnants of empire to a few, very small islands under British, Dutch and French control (though, in a formal sense, the French territories are not colonies, but instead are integral parts of France). Britain, The Netherlands, France, and to a lesser extent Spain – the four European states with the most important historic ties to the Caribbean, dating back to 1492 And All That – continue to have a 'presence' in the region; so, increasingly does the European Community (EC); and since 1960, a European power with no historic ties to the region, the USSR, has also been a significant player. I propose first to look at the remnants of empire under the control of Britain, The Netherlands and France, and then to consider Europe's relations with the independent states of the region, including the activities of Spain, the EC, and the USSR. I shall be concerned essentially with the three decades since 1960.

REMNANTS OF EMPIRE: BRITAIN

Since 1945, in the context of a general transfer of global hegemony from Britain to the USA, formal decolonisation was the UK's objective in the Caribbean, albeit at London's pace and on its own terms. With the collapse of the Federation of the West Indies, decolonisation was accelerated, but now on an island'basis. After 1960 London's 'policy' (if it deserved such a term) was to grant independence to each colony as and when its government so requested. The four largest countries got independence between 1962 and 1966 (Jamaica, Trinidad & Tobago, Barbados, Guyana), despite much political turmoil and ethnic conflict in Guyana in those years. By Act of

Parliament in 1967, 'Associated Statehood' was granted to the OECS islands; in effect, this was internal self-government with London retaining control of foreign affairs, defence and security. The only real difficulty was presented by Anguilla, which seceded from the Associated State of St. Kitts-Nevis. London sent troops and police in 1969, and Anguilla was returned to full Crown Colony status as a separate unit.

By the early 1970s, London had decided that total disengagement (the grant of full independence once a duly elected government asked for it) was its most economic option. Hence Grenada went that route despite the bitter opposition to independence under Gairy; then Dominica, St. Lucia, St. Vincent, Antigua and St. Kitts-Nevis. Belize presented a problem because of the long-standing territorial dispute with Guatemala; but independence was granted in 1981 with an agreement to keep a permanent British garrison there indefinitely.

By 1981 therefore, as today, Britain had only five colonial dependencies in the Caribbean, all very small: Anguilla, Montserrat, British Virgin Islands, Cayman Islands, Turks and Caicos. They total about 400 square miles and their population is some 65,000 (about a quarter of that of the Netherlands Antilles and Aruba). They are literally the rocks on which Britain's hopes for complete disengagement in the Caribbean have floundered; and they floundered because these islands' leaders and population refused the independence option. London hardly had anything as grand as a 'policy' for these little colonies, especially so far as their political future was concerned, though their per capita incomes were relatively high in the 1980s because of expanding tourism and their role as tax havens and drug transshipment points.

In 1985–86 events in the Turks and Caicos made London pay some attention; the increasing use of these islands as a drug transit centre led to the arrest of the Chief Minister in Miami, which prompted Britain to impose a constitutional change to allow the governor to rule through an appointed Council. There was a re-assessment of policy towards the remaining colonies, and consensus that Britain would not push them to independence, but would try to upgrade the local administrations until the public seemed more clearly in favour of it. The premise was now (and is still) that British rule would continue for the foreseeable future. Only in Montserrat is there significant support for independence, and even here it is hardly overwhelming. Britain also continues its fairly significant military presence in Belize and its diplomatic efforts to solve the Guatemala dispute. Recent developments suggest that a resolution is imminent. Belize and Guatemala are now poised to sign a definitive treaty, and one might assume that this will signal British disengagement, with the USA as the de facto guarantor of Belizean national integrity. Interestingly though, very recently a British military commander was quoted as saying that he hoped that the troops would stay in Belize because it was such a good place to train soldiers. It seems the remnants of empire still have their uses.

REMNANTS OF EMPIRE: THE NETHERLANDS

For The Netherlands, Indonesia was always the most important colony by a long way; it won its independence in 1949 after a bloody struggle. This left Suriname, and the Netherlands Antilles (NA), consisting of six islands: Curaçao, Aruba and Bonaire off Venezuela (the ABC Islands), and St. Marten (half of the island), St. Eustatius (Statia) and Saba in the Leewards. In 1954, the Charter of the Kingdom of The Netherlands constituted Suriname and the NA 'autonomous partners' with Holland in the 'Tripartite Kingdom'. In a formal sense this was seen as an end to colonial status as well as a step to full independence. Only defence and foreign affairs were reserved to The Hague, and future changes in the Charter would require the consent of all three 'partners'.

After 1954 independence was not high on anyone's agenda, until events in 1969 and the early 1970s. In 1969 there was political instability in both Suriname and Curaçao; in the latter, serious riots led to the entry of Dutch troops to 'restore order' under Article 43 of the Charter. Suriname moved to independence in 1975, with massive Dutch aid (around US $3,000 per capita) and free emigration to Holland (150,000 had moved there by 1976, about one-third of the population). This left the six-island NA within the Kingdom. The Dutch government encouraged them to move towards independence too, but their politicians resisted; a growing separatist movement in Aruba also complicated matters.

These are very small islands. The total population was about 248,000 in 1985, with 147,000 in Curaçao, 68,000 in Aruba, and fewer than 1000 in Saba (all of 13 square kilometers). Moreover, 600 miles of ocean separate the ABC islands from the others. After very long negotiations in the early 1980s, Aruba received separate status as an autonomous partner in the Kingdom in 1986, with the understanding that it would move to full independence in 1996. The other five islands stayed together as the NA, also within the Kingdom, and have not committed themselves to any constitutional change leading to independence. Development aid to the NA is relatively generous, and this, along with the oil industry in Curaçao and Aruba, results in a standard of living which is high by Caribbean standards. All inhabitants have Dutch passports and rights to free migration and full social benefits in Holland, where well over 60,000 Antilleans now live.

But there is much uncertainty about the future status of the NA and Aruba. The example of Suriname is discouraging: massive out-migration up to 1980, coups, military terror, Maroon insurgency, civil war, continued military intervention even after the elections of 1987, economic disasters, suspension of Dutch aid after the murder of opposition leaders in 1982, increasing drugs transshipment allegedly involving the military. Antillean leaders doubt that their islands can survive alone, especially with the crisis in the oil industry. The great majority of the people oppose weakening constitutional ties with

Holland, but the French option of full integration is also rejected both in the islands and in Holland. Strictly, the NA and Aruba are not colonies under the Charter, and the UN recognises this (Holland is not required to report on the islands each year as colonial powers are). They have full internal self-government and in foreign relations are included in relevant negotiations, treaties and so on. But Article 43 makes The Hague the guarantor of internal order and external security in the islands (hence the 1969 intervention in Curaçao), and this is a source of anxiety on both sides of the Atlantic, especially granted the increasing likelihood that the islands may be used as drugs transfer points.

There is no support at present for full, total independence, not even in Aruba, and the consensus seems to be for a sort of 'commonwealth' which would really continue the status quo under a different name. There is concern about relations within the NA; there is considerable overlapping jurisdictions as between the federal unit and the five island authorities; and there is some pressure towards further fragmentation, especially from Curaçao. Total disengagement is impossible, even if the Dutch wanted it; decolonisation in this context would be an arbitrary, colonial act. What may result is a 'Commonwealth' with four autonomous partners: Holland, Aruba (which looks as if it will not opt for independence in 1996); Curaçao with Bonaire; the three smaller islands. Within the last few days (March 1992) meetings took place between the Dutch Prime Minister and the politicians of the NA and Aruba to try to reach some kind of agreement along these lines. As with the British dependencies, a formal Dutch presence in the Caribbean seems destined to continue well into the 1990s.

REMNANTS OF EMPIRE: FRANCE

In 1946, France's 'old colonies' in the Caribbean became 'Departments d'Outre-Mer' (DOMs): Martinique, Guadeloupe with its small island dependencies of St. Martin (the other half), St. Barts, Les Saintes and Marie Galante, and French Guiana or Cayenne. (The fourth DOM is Reunion in the Indian Ocean). This ended formal French colonialism in the Caribbean with a stroke of the pen. DOMs are not colonies, they are not overseas territories like the French islands in the Pacific; they are fully integrated parts of France, governed by the same departmental structure as the rest of the country. Yet France has not been able to resolve the ambiguities and doubts about the three Caribbean DOMs.

How have they fared since 1946? The DOMs come under the social welfare legislation of metropolitan France. By the 1980s, wages, welfare provisions, health services were all excellent by OECS standards, although the comparison which interested the Antilleans was with France, and every remaining difference in benefits was resented. Because the DOMs are poorer than the metropolitan departments, more is actually spent on social expenditure per

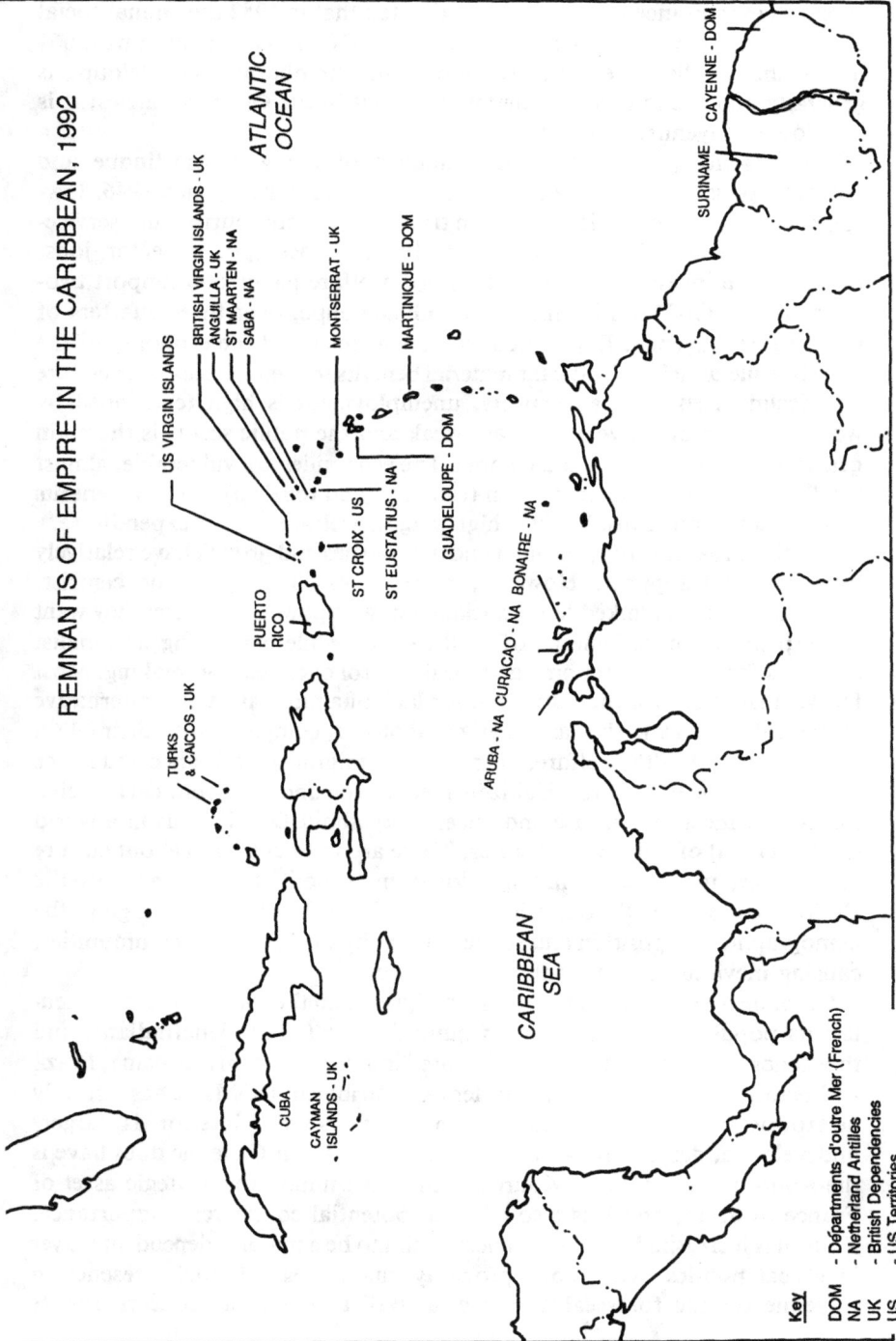

REMNANTS OF EMPIRE IN THE CARIBBEAN, 1992

ATLANTIC OCEAN

CARIBBEAN SEA

US VIRGIN ISLANDS

BRITISH VIRGIN ISLANDS - UK
ANGUILLA - UK
ST MAARTEN - NA
SABA - NA

MONTSERRAT - UK

MARTINIQUE - DOM

GUADELOUPE - DOM

ST CROIX - US

ST EUSTATIUS - NA

ARUBA - NA CURACAO - NA BONAIRE - NA

PUERTO RICO

TURKS & CAICOS - UK

CUBA

CAYMAN ISLANDS - UK

SURINAME CAYENNE - DOM

Key

DOM - Départments d'outre Mer (French)
NA   - Netherland Antilles
UK   - British Dependencies
US   - US Territories

capita than in France proper; it was estimated that in 1982 the annual social expenditure per capita was 1539 francs in the DOMs as compared with 661 in the metropolis. The infrastructure in Martinique and Guadeloupe is generally good, and certainly better than that in the OECS countries; it is inferior in Cayenne.

There is no question that the standard of living in Martinque and Guadeloupe is high in comparison with the OECS states. Since 1946, low-wage plantation economies have been transformed into tourism and service-based economies. Transfer payments from France (public sector jobs, metropolitan investment in infrastructure, welfare payments) support two-thirds of the GNP in Martinique and Guadeloupe, over three-quarters of the GNP in Cayenne. Department status has distorted the economy of the DOMs while bringing significant material benefits to their citizens: Agriculture has declined, so have all exports, unemployment is high (cushioned by welfare), the productive sectors are weak and the public sector is the main generator of employment and income. The economies are vulnerable, almost totally dependent on metropolitan transfers (and tourism); but the benefits to individuals are considerable: high wages, welfare, social expenditure.

For these reasons, the pro-independence parties and groups have relatively little electoral support. However, there is much support for centrist, autonomist parties, linked to the socialists now in power in France; they want to keep the material benefits of DOM status while expressing nationalist demands for greater autonomy and local control over decision-making. Most DOM citizens opt for the status quo for lack of a more attractive alternative in the real world, and they are clearly well placed, compared with their OECS neighbours, in health, welfare, mobility (free migration to France and hence anywhere in the EC as French citizens), education and even political and civil rights. Yet most feel unease and uncertainty about DOM status in a world (and a region) of independent states. There are valid concerns about culture and dignity; and increased immigration of metropolitan Frenchmen into the DOMs, coupled with out-migration by local blacks, is changing the demographic composition and social geography of these small communities, causing inevitable resentments and anxieties.

Cayenne is very different. It is much bigger than the islands; it is continen-tal; its population composition is quite distinct (many Amerindians, and thousands of recent and still unassimilated immigrants from Suriname, Brazil and Haiti); it is poorer than the other two Caribbean DOMs; it has virtually no tourism; its infrastructure is inferior; its vast interior is largely undeveloped, despite sporadic efforts by Paris. What Cayenne does have is the Kourou Space Centre. Kourou is the most important strategic asset of France overseas, and it is also of great potential commercial importance. Kourou is increasingly vital to France's claim to be a major independent player in global politics. This alone probably guarantees a French presence in Cayenne for the foreseeable future, as well as mounting concern for its security, especially with near-chaos in next-door Suriname threatening to spill over. No such strategic asset exists in Martinique or Guadeloupe; but French prestige and historic ties, along with investment in tourism and other sectors, make it most unlikely that France will pressure the DOMs towards independence. Nor does it seem likely at present that opinion within the Caribbean DOMs will swing decisively around to that option.

RELATIONS WITH INDEPENDENT STATES: THE OLD COLONIAL POWERS

Britain, The Netherlands and France have tried to maintain 'special relations' with their former colonies when these became independent, to varying degrees. In the 1960s and 1970s, Britain assigned very low priority to the Caribbean in her foreign policy, but the embarrassment of the US invasion of Grenada in 1983 prompted a re-appraisal, and a more active Caribbean policy. Since then Britain has engaged more fully with the CARICOM states, in relation to trade, private sector investment, aid, and technical co-operation, which in recent times has extended to OECS security, help to the Trinidad & Tobago police force, and aid and advice on drugs interdiction.

France has maintained close ties with Haiti, the largest francophone state in the region. To its discredit, Paris tended to support the Duvaliers uncritically, but since the ouster of 'Baby Doc' it has been more active with respect to economic and cultural aid. In 1988, France was the second biggest aid donor to Haiti, after the USA, and France sponsored Haiti's entry to the African, Caribbean and Pacific (ACP) grouping for the Lome IV negotiations. French diplomats have played a high-profile role since the military coup which ousted Aristide last year. France has also cultivated relations (under the idea of 'francophonie', the community of nations in the world which speak French) with the Creole-speaking islands of St. Lucia and Dominica since their independence, giving bilateral aid and cultural support. Other than these ties, France has little interest in the Caribbean, except the DOMs, of course.

The Netherlands has maintained a presence in Suriname since its independence in 1975. The Dutch have tried to influence Surinamese governments by suspending or reinstating aid and by informal contacts; large numbers of Surinamese live in Holland, including political exiles of one kind or another. These attempts to manipulate political life in Suriname (with the blessing of the USA) seem likely to continue, and they cause less resentment than similar ploys by Washington would do.

Spain, the original colonial power, has also tried to develop special ties with her former colonies in the region, although her relations with Latin America proper have always been more important to her. But Cuba has occupied a special place in Spanish foreign policy since 1959. High-level visits take place, both ways; Spain was the first EC state to receive Castro officially as Head of State (not until 1990, however). Solid commercial ties with Cuba were forged in the 1960s. In 1986, Cuba imported 15 per cent of all Spanish exports to Latin America and was Spain's single biggest market in the western hemisphere. Madrid in recent years (with a socialist government) has tried to pressure Castro to deepen his dialogue with Latin American leaders and to modify his political and economic system, not, it must be said, with much success, and Cuba has refused to participate in any of the 1992 events sponsored by Spain. The Dominican Republic, Spain's oldest colony anywhere, was sponsored by Madrid for entry to the ACP group for the Lome IV negotiations. Madrid also encourages Santo Domingo to take a foreign policy line more independent of Washington, and is heavily involved in the lavish celebrations of 1492 in the Dominican Republic. It has a hand in Puerto Rican 1992 events too, and Puerto Rico has a 'mission' in Madrid despite its status vis-a-vis the USA; Spanish investment, especially in banking, has increased considerably in Puerto Rico in recent years. Overall though, the Caribbean as opposed to Latin America has been relatively unimportant in Spain's foreign policy since the fall of Franco in the 1970s, and Madrid has tended to look to multi-lateral relations with the independent states, especially within the framework of the EC.

The EC itself has become increasingly important to the region as a source of trade and aid. The British and Dutch dependencies have the status of 'Overseas Countries and Territories' and receive aid as such; most of it goes to the NA and Aruba, with about four times the population of the British islands. The independent states are part of the ACP group (that is, the CARICOM countries, Suriname, and very recently Haiti and the Dominican Republic) and receive trade and aid concessions under the Lome Conventions. These concessions have been useful for all these states since the 1970s, and especially important for the less developed countries of the OECS, particularly the EC support for banana and sugar exports under special protocols. (These may now be in jeopardy with the change to the single market scheduled for the end of 1992). The French DOMs come fully under the Treaty of Rome as a part of France, and they benefit from aid far in excess of what they could have received as independent states under the Lome Conventions.

RELATIONS WITH INDEPENDENT STATES: THE USSR

The USSR is (or rather, was) a country with absolutely no historic ties to the Caribbean situated 6000 miles from the region. Yet its involvement in the Caribbean since 1960 has had the greatest impact of all in terms of international relations, from the missile crisis of 1962 to the Grenada invasion in 1983. Moscow developed close links to Cuba from 1960, the year after Castro took power. Military aid was stepped up after the Bay of Pigs and Castro's official conversion to Marxist-Leninist ideology, while direct aid, artificial prices for Cuban sugar and heavily subsidised oil and manufactured goods from the Eastern bloc, ensured that Cuba's entire economy became heavily dependent on the USSR.

For Kruschev, Soviet prestige globally was tied to the survival of the Cuban Revolution. Offensive missiles were stationed in Cuba not so much to defend the island as to redress the global strategic balance of power in favour of Moscow. By agreement, the Cuban territory on which the missiles were deployed was to be under total Soviet control. Kruschev did not consult with Castro during the negotiations with Washington in 1962 which led to a US commitment not to invade Cuba and the removal of the missiles; Castro was (justifiably) infuriated at his exclusion, just as he was last year (1991) at the unilateral Soviet decision to withdraw all its troops from the island. The 1962 crisis taught that the USSR would not risk its security to defend the Cuban Revolution and that superpower relations were far more important to Moscow than any Third World client state, even a much favoured one like Cuba. It also taught that the USA would not permit an outside power to establish an offensive military capacity in the Caribbean, even if Washington would learn to live with the Cuban regime itself (though never, up to 1992, relaxing its trade embargo or ending its general harassment of the regime).

Cuba continued to be a major beneficiary of Soviet aid in the post-Kruschev era, and continued support was tied up with Soviet prestige in global politics. But the relationship was not without tensions. While Cuba had been expelled from the OAS and was trying to export revolution to Latin America by aiding guerilla movements, Moscow was anxious to develop better relations with the OAS states and eschewed support for the armed Left. As Cuba became increasingly dependent economically on the Soviet bloc, Moscow was able to bring Castro into line in the late 1960s, though he continued at times to take an independent stand on foreign policy. In the 1970s Cuba became fully integrated into the Soviet economic bloc and it was the only state in the western hemisphere to be a member of COMECON.

In the 1970s, too, Moscow cultivated relations with the new Caribbean states — Guyana, Jamaica, Trinidad & Tobago, Suriname after 1975, Grenada after 1979 — but it gave them very little aid, preferring to concentrate on Third World states defined as important in geo-strategic terms. The Caribbean, after all, was clearly in the US sphere, Cuba or no Cuba. Aid on ideological grounds to pro-socialist governments like Michael Manley's and Forbes Burnham's in the 1970s was low-key; Soviet trade with Jamaica increased after 1980 when Seaga came to power.

At first, Moscow showed little interest in the 1979 coup which established the People's Revolutionary Government (PRG) in Grenada. Even later, the documentary evidence shows how reluctant and grudging Soviet support really was, even though the PRG acquired all the trappings and rhetoric of a Soviet-type political system and consistently voted for the USSR in the UN. Unlike

Cuba, Grenada was never integrated into the Soviet bloc and it never received significant Soviet development aid or trade concessions. The evidence makes it clear that Moscow attached little importance to the Grenada regime and had no plans to use it to export revolution to the Caribbean. The USSR did conclude two secret military agreements with the PRG in 1980 and 1982, but the equipment provided was modest. No Soviet troops were stationed in Grenada, and there is no evidence of an attempt to turn the island into a naval or air base or to build a massive military machine with which to destabilise the Eastern Caribbean (or elsewhere). Brezhnev had no wish to embroil his troubled giant of a country, in the early 1980s, in yet another costly Caribbean adventure.

The Gorbachev era (1985–91) has seen Moscow assuming a far lower profile in the Third World. In the Caribbean, this has meant decreasing aid to Cuba, even though it was part of the socialist bloc, and pressuring Castro to reform its economic system. As the USSR began to disintegrate these trends accelerated dramatically. In 1991 Moscow announced (with no prior consultation with Havana) that it would immediately begin to withdraw all its troops in the island, amounting to several thousand. Castro did not conceal his contempt for Gorbachev and his regime (he publicly supported the counter-Gorbachev coup in August 1991) or his anger at the new policies towards Cuba. His relationship with Moscow is now close to crisis point. As the USSR disappears, the successor republics, including Russia, are certain to turn inward, and full disengagement from Cuba now seems likely, with unpredictable consequences for the Castro regime and the Cuban people. Russian impact on the Caribbean generally is likely to be minimal in the next decade, short of some extraordinary development in the former Soviet Union.

The presence of the other European states, however, seems certain to continue through the next decade and beyond: the formal dependencies, the DOMs, trade and aid and investment, whether through the EC or bilateral, all guarantee this. It seems unlikely that Britain, The Netherlands or France will disengage from their formal responsibilities even if these may be reduced, as in Belize. Indeed, concerns about drugs and regional security may even see some increase in Britain and Dutch involvement (with US blessing, of course). And informal contacts and influences are, of course, very important: these include history, language, culture, religion, systems of law and government, international relations, international organisations (such as the Commonwealth or Socialist International), education, sports, and much more. Europe will continue to play a part in Caribbean affairs as we move to the twenty-first century, though no longer the hegemonic Powers in the region that they were for most of the post-Columbian half millenium.

SUGGESTIONS FOR FURTHER READING

De Kadt, E. (ed.), *Patterns of Foreign Influence in the Caribbean* (Oxford University Press, Oxford, 1972).

Knight, Franklin, *The Caribbean. The Genesis of a Fragmented Nationalism. Second Edition* (Oxford University Press, New York, 1990).

Knight, Franklin and Palmer, Colin (eds.), *The Modern Caribbean* (University of North Carolina Press, Chapel Hill and London, 1989).

Sutton, P. (ed.), *Europe and the Caribbean* (University of Warwick Press and Macmillan, London, 1991); This book has an excellent bibliography on the different territories and colonial linkages mentioned in the paper.

6

European Stereotypes and the Position of Women in the Caribbean: An Historical Overview

KATHLEEN PHILLIPS-LEWIS

She is cautious, gorgeous and also glorious
And marvellous
She is delightful to meet and delectable
And adorable
She is a dew drop as any one can tell
Elusive as the Scarlet Pimpernel
With a handy little figure and cheek of rose
Delicate fingers and pointed toes.

G. Rohlehr. *Calypso and Society* in Pre-independence Trinidad (1990).

In the above quoted calypso coming out of Trinidad society of the 1930s, the calypsonian, the Roaring Lion, sings praises of the ideal woman with whom he is 'Happy to be in Love'. The most interesting thing about this occurrence, as Gordon Rohlehr points out, is that she is *white*, not unlike all other idealized types in calypso and other fictional and literary forms of the Caribbean during this era and before. The Roaring Lion's beloved is as European as they come, exhibiting all the virtues, physical and otherwise, of the romanticized Victorian Lady, except that she has the Caribbean kaiso 'rhythm in her waist'. The European stereotype of the 'genteel society' of the nineteenth century was slowly becoming Caribbeanized, but almost imperceptibly. Then, suddenly, in the eighties a new ideal type hits centre stage, having shed her blond, rosy, delicate European respectability. Now she is David Michael Rudder's 'Bacchanal Lady', the woman who is truly Caribbean, who is 'neither here nor there' but everywhere, who is a superb mix of 'sweet scandal' and 'real magic', the woman who rules the Carnival and who will 'mix your milk with puncheon rum', for she is neither Madonna nor Magdalen but a combination of both in equal blends, no longer prepared to immolate herself at the altar of eternal self-sacrifice for the sake of respectability and acceptability as dictated by Victorian society. As

David Rudder puts it, our Caribbean Lady is now prepared to 'infect you with her ramajay' while taking 'your status symbol high away', she'd rather project her true indigenous self than pursue the 'rum and coca cola' type lifestyles and value systems of the outside world.

The story seems to be that the Caribbean woman has either been transformed over time or that images and perceptions of the Caribbean woman have undergone radical reconstruction over the years. 'Bacchanal Lady' is herself a contradiction in terms, in the Victorian sense. What this indicates is that both views are relevant; 1) the Caribbean woman has liberated herself from the social shackles and stays which hemmed her in, and, 2) that society has liberated her from the stereotypical strait jacket hitherto prescribed to keep her 'in her place'.

The question now arises how far reaching is this transformation and how has it been achieved? This paper will address itself to these questions with an examination of the transference of Victorian gender stereotypes to the Caribbean. It will be illustrated that over 500 years of post-Columbian history, the Caribbean woman has had to struggle against internalizing such stereotypical notions about herself, against giving the nod to the European 'see-what-I-mean' mentality. The struggle has been an uphill one in which many bit the dust and many battles were lost, but also in which many victories were won — the cumulative result being the emergence of a new and free Caribbean woman fully cognizant of all possibilities open to her and anxious to explore them all.

The one constant throughout her history, through the mountains and valleys of her historical experiences, has been the remarkable resilience of the Caribbean woman. It is this resilience which has allowed her to survive 500 years of discrimination and to hold on to all that she is and ever fought to be; to be strong, to be the slave, the concubine, the indentured labourer, the peasant, the small-scale own-account agriculturist, the huckster, the higgler, the cane cutter, the matriarch, the social worker, the reformer, the spiritual mother, the educator, the rebel, the political and labour activist, the professional career woman, the prostitute, the jamette. It was this last Caribbean type who truly reversed, as Bridget Brereton puts it, 'the canons of respectability, the norms of the superstructure with her bravery, her wit ... her talent in song and dance, her indifference to the law, her sexual prowess', and all of this during the nineteenth century when the Victorian 'Angel of the House' ideal was riding the waves of popularity at home and abroad.

The Caribbean woman, throughout her history, has been all of these things and more, the mother, the daughter, the sister, the sweetheart, the lover, the friend, and not forgetting the criminal, the accomplice, the enemy, the traitor, even the pirate and the buccaneer. In defiance of superimposed stereotypes, the Caribbean woman has proven herself equally capable of using her most 'feminine charms' to hypnotize, captivate and mamaguy, as of seizing the reins when necessary, wearing the pants and taking full control both in the private and the public spheres. Yet, until quite recently the Caribbean woman had been, and in many respects continues to be, the unsung and unheralded heroine. While, therefore, she has covered a laudable distance along the road to full liberation and equality, the fight is far from over. In many respects she continues to be stigmatized by nineteenth century European gender role stereotypes. In fact, even before the Victorian era, Caribbean women have been judged and misjudged by European yardsticks, dating back to the time when Europeans first set foot on these shores five hundred years ago and claimed these lands for the Queen and for God. Apparently, God had been, until then, oblivious to their existence, and therefore must be thanking the Europeans for having introduced Him to the Caribbean peoples. This is the God whom Europeans depict in their own image as being white and, above all, male.

EUROPEAN GENDER STEREOTYPES

In order to understand the struggle of Caribbean women against stereotyping, we must first understand the essence and origin of the stereotypical images themselves, the very images which are transmitted in virtually unmodified fashion from 'the mother country' to the colonies, the very images which were used to polarize the sexes in Europe and to define a woman's rightful place and keep her there.

In their attempt to challenge die-hard notions of male political, economic, socio-cultural and, above all, natural hegemony, European feminists have exhibited a definite enthusiasm and interest in uncovering their past. They came to realise that woman's virtual absence from the annals of European and other history was not indicative of her lack of accomplishment, achievement or involvement, not because she had done nothing, but because what she had done, her thoughts, her activities, were not considered worthwhile topics for historical analysis and documentation. Like working class and racial minorities, women were merely another subjugated group, too ordinary to have contributed in any significant way to building the foundations of civilisation. An examination of the lives of such ordinary people was deemed, as Sheila Rowbotham puts it, 'beneath the dignity of history'.

The process of rediscovery revealed that woman had a past, and that hers was as active an involvement in erecting the edifice of modern society as man's. There had always been some form of gender discrimination in societies of ancient times; legal and political subordination are evident in the teachings of Christianity, in Roman and Greek mythology as well as in classical antiquity, but it did not always nor necessarily bring with it economic passivity and dependence nor a total separation of the spheres over which each sex exercised influence and control.

In fact, prior to the rise of the Victorian industrial middle class, European women of every walk of life were heavily involved in economic activity, their involvement being determined by their need to survive and to ensure the survival of their families. Her reproductive function did not hinder nor restrict her economic productive capacity. Real women in Medieval Europe, for instance, whether she was a noblewoman, a peasant or a bourgeois, undertook the same tasks as the men of their class.

Ladies of the manor were not the pampered creatures of the later imposed stereotypes. In fact, with her husband away so often fighting wars and crusades, she shouldered the entire burden of managing the household, the estate and the serfs, in addition to which she had to settle disputes, practise medicine, and defend the castle and lands in case of attacks.

Peasant women undertook all the daily routine tasks of farming: running the dairy, brewing the ale, gardening, shearing sheep, harvesting crops, spinning, carding, weaving and ploughing.

Middle class women worked in traditionally male skilled areas, as apothecaries, barbers, jewellers, traders, shopkeepers, masons, bakers, tailors, silkworkers, blacksmiths. Then there were those who entered the medical professions as midwives, doctors, surgeons, and nurses; there were the professional artists and painters, carvers and sculptoresses, musicians and troubadors, writers, poets and teachers.

The European woman of pre-industrial times had always been the 'yokefellow' or 'helpmeet' of her male counterpart. Her labour was in fact 'equal to, if not greater than, a man's'. But all of these women became posthumous victims of the Victorian middle class stereotypes which were applied backwards into time, distorting, marginalising, delegitimising and even negating the historical experience of half of humanity.

The change came, first to Britain, with the Agricultural Revolution, which defined a major advance, a quantum leap forward in the modernisation of human existence. Mechanisation and capitalisation of farming produced agricultural surplusses, releasing surplus hands from toil and thus breaking up the old agrarian type community and family units of social organisation. The declining need for full family involvement in agricultural production led gradually to a definite gender division of labour and to the increasing 'housewifisation' of middle class women. The image of the woman as a creature of 'ceaseless toil' was gradually being transformed into that of a creature of 'ceaseless leisure'. Such middle class notions were eventually generalised in their application to women of all social classes, thus negating the ongoing experience of working class women who continued to toil in obscurity, oppression and abject poverty.

The Industrial Revolution served to polarize further the distinction between sex roles by concretizing the sexual division of labour and thus formalizing, once and for all, the ideology of 'separate spheres'. Girls were trained for leisured lives, and to fulfil their natural roles and assume their rightful place as wives and mothers, carers, bearers and rearers strictly within the domestic/private sphere, while boys were afforded academic education to equip them for their future tasks of managing the economy, organising the society, running the state and supervising the imperial effort. Patriarchal authority came to be clearly defined both in the home and in public life, and was underwritten by legislation, constitution, social attitudes and intellectual pronouncements. By the Victorian era, women had been fully relegated to historical obscurity through the 'silence of sex'. Victorian stereotypes merely reinforced the received notions inherited from earlier times and refind them to their glorious apogee.

The stereotypical ideal of Victorian womanhood was that she was 'sugar and spice and everything nice', 'the masterpiece of myth and fantasy', superior to man morally and spiritually, but inferior to him in intellect and personality. She was thus garlanded with 'the stainless sceptre' and halo of influential motherhood, lauded for her physical charms but denied capacity for sexual enjoyment. Her economic role was confined to 'conspicuous consumption', her social role to the artistic and the ornamental. The ideal of Victorian womanhood was the middle and upper class woman, while the working class woman was considered less than human, and therefore, hardly deserving of the appellation 'woman' at all except by unavoidable biological happenstance.

The middle class, itself a product of the new industrial economic order, had become caught up in a struggle to map out for itself its own rightful place, its own niche in this new society — a niche fitting of its new material status and wealth, its newly acquired political ascendancy. It became important, therefore, to delimit the boundaries between its present and past social status as between the 'genteel folk' and the under classes, whom they viewed with no small amount of contempt. Part and parcel of this need for socio-cultural distance was the assumption of new value systems, a polished veneer of spirituality and religiosity as well as a new morality, a new view of woman's role.

This society, now suddenly seized by divine afflatus, devised for itself quaint sexual mores aimed at resurrecting the ideals of ascetic chastity, celibacy and prudery, thus channelling the relationship between the sexes along more respectable and acceptable lines. The outcome was the development of what Carl Degler called 'a double standard of sexual morality' which necessitated the suppression and, albeit, outright denial of female sexuality. Wives were expected to submit themselves dutifully to their husbands, not for their own sexual gratification or pleasure but out of a sense of obligation and for the purpose of procreation. Wives were instructed to 'lie still and think of the Empire'. One standard obtained for the bedroom and another for the living room; one for the male and another for the female; one for the upper classes and another for the working class. It was hoped that, for the middle class madonnas, sex would be dematerialized by silence. While the Victorian Lady was expected to 'glide through life like an elegant swan ... untroubled by the lusts of the flesh', the lower class 'fallen woman' was to be her sexual surrogate. In her role as 'the hired instrument of masculine pleasure', the working class prostitute provided a valuable service, meeting the demands of a multi-faceted clientele ranging from the 'unbridled passions of precocious youth' to the 'deviant desires of vicious men'. Only good, respectable women were assumed to be asexual and Victorians strove for goodness and respectability.

The sexual or rather asexual stereotype was not the only one under which

Victorian women and colonial women had to struggle. The married woman was further idealized in her role as wife and was therefore beseeched from all quarters with an abundance of well-meant advice about the performance of her bridal function. A wife had to be truly dignified in person, carriage and bearing. She had to be humble, dependent, self-abased, unobtrusive, quiet, impartially polite to all, totally devoted to her husband and children and 'willing to bend to circumstances' for his sake.

A woman's inferior status was further underscored by the findings and theories of learned nineteenth century scientists: biologists, anthropologists, sociologists, physicians, all of whom sanctioned the notion that she was a naturally inferior being 'shaped by an ineluctable evolutionary process into a form that could not have been altered' by wishful thinking, education, nor legislation. As far as education and productive employment were concerned, she was not expected to compete with the male of her species, for he was the more resourceful and energetic of the two. Already hampered by physical impediments, her resources were further depleted by constant menstruation and childbirth, thus hindering her progress along the evolutionary road on par with her male counterpart. Patrick Geddes and Arthur Thompson (*The Evolution of Sex,* London, 1914) advanced the theory that sexual functions were determined by metabolism: the relatively more anabolic was the female, while the male was relatively more katabolic, which meant in effect that it was metabolic ratios which imbued the female with the 'more constructive processes' (e.g. her child-bearing capacity). Women felt more and had more 'rapid intuition' and were naturally more passive, while men thought more, possessed more judgement and scientific insight and were more active. To add insult to injury, women were cautioned not to worry about such imbalances because, in effect, the two sexes complemented each other.

Intellectually, too, women were inferior, their brain weight being 5 ounces less than the man's. The man therefore was thought to be capable of higher, more original levels of intellectual work, while the woman's long suit lay in 'the higher evolution of her sensory organs'. She was therefore more given to fickleness, highly charged emotional displays, passionate scenes and craved emotional excitement 'of all kinds', while men were governed by the 'restraint of reason', tenacity of purpose, stability of mental constitution and determination to overcome all obstacles. Such natural differences, therefore, made men more suited to intellectual pursuits such as literary criticism and scientific inquiry while women excelled in matters of 'aesthetic emotion' and 'feminine taste' such as interior decorating, floral arrangement and colour coordination and dress sense.

Education, it follows, was not a domain or privilege designed for women. Higher education not only had disastrous effects on the woman herself but also on her offspring and, by extension, on her entire society. Diversion of her life force and her productive energies into academic pursuits rather than the business of reproduction, had the negative effect of reducing her fertility, diminishing her lactation capacity as well as seriously restricting her offspring and her own chances of survival and a healthy, normal existence. Distinguished men in society were all found to be the sons of devoted stay-at-home mothers who had sufficient intellectual capability to excel in the academic field, but who had chosen instead to exert their energies in their traditional functions. Women were therefore advised to choose babies over books, for the sake of all concerned. Incidentally, the originator of such theories, T.S. Clouston, was knighted for his contributions in the field of medical research.

The sum total of such stereotypical notions of ideal womanhood was that Home was clearly woman's intended place, and domestic arts, graces and skills her fitting domain. Given her passionate rather than rational inclinations, she was deemed to have no business in the world of religious leadership, industrial pursuits nor political machination. The male was better equipped for the cut-throat competitive fields. The public/political sphere was indeed a 'man's world'. The woman was to be protected and kept safe within the private/domestic sphere, while in return she was expected to keep the home fires warm and to maintain peace and tranquility at home, providing a welcome sanctuary for her husband to return to after a hard day in the 'dog-eat-dog' world of bread-winning and political jockeying out there. Even within the home, as the stereotypes indicate, she could exercise influence, but never authority nor power. In the business of reproduction, too, her role was secondary and incidental: she was considered never an active participant but merely a receptacle for sexual reproduction, 'the carriers of the fetuses created by men'. On every count, then, polarized ideas of human nature relegated the woman to a position decidedly inferior or 'female', while men were undoubtedly superior or 'male'. These were the stereotypes which were handed down, either through inadvertence or intent and design to colonial society.

GENDER STEREOTYPES AND THE EMPIRE: TRANSFERRENCE TO THE CARIBBEAN

The late nineteenth century saw the beginning of the age of 'High Imperialism' when the industrialized nations of Europe sallied forth to conquer the world and make it a better place for all humanity, at least so the European version of the story goes. This was the Victorian era; it was a time when the division of labour abounded in industrialised countries and when gender differences were used to assign tasks, the 'less desirable and remunerative ... to people stigmatized as inferior'. The idea of female inferiority and male superiority was transported to the colonial setting with the imperialists, the administrators, the reformers, the explorers and adventurers, the traders and capitalists from Europe. In the first instance, European women and wives living in the colonies were assigned role and function based upon such stereotypical assumptions. These women were expected to make themselves useful as care-givers, educators, and hostesses rather than administrators, military personnel, professionals and officials (even planters). Interestingly enough, as Margaret Strobel points out, the patriarchal ideology was even extended to the relationship between the imperial power and the colonies, the former being seen as 'the mother country' and the latter the 'immature and untrained children', thus attempting to mask the fact of exploitation.

Similarly, occupying the underdog position, wives within the European communities were kept at a safe social distance from the local peoples in order to protect them from the sexual appetites of local men, given their extreme vulnerability. As at home, these wives were expected to keep themselves pure, chaste, faithful and inviolable and to exist in blissful oblivion to their husband's possession of concubines of local origin. In the colonial setting during the age of high imperialism, as in the plantation era notions of female inferiority were extended to include racial, ethnic and colour categories. Women who belonged to the non-white races suffered therefore double inferiority: by race and by gender, inferior to European male as well as European female. Such divisive structures and ideologies were not applied uniquely to African and Asiatic peoples during the late 19th and early 20th centuries, but as John Hobson puts it, to all peoples of the 'lower races' everywhere and at other times throughout history, (such as the pre-Columbian indigenous peoples of the New World who were enslaved, exploited and their women raped and sexually exploited from the time of Columbus onward). These women were considered inferior as regards gender, race, colour, class, culture and place of origin. It is interesting that whenever European feminists analyze the impact of imperialism on gender relations, they consider, in the main, the relationships between the sexes of those of European origin, i.e. of the colonizers rather than the colonized or between colonizer and colonized. Colonial peoples in general, whether viewed from a feminist perspective or not by those of imperialist nations, at least until recently were viewed as acted upon rather than as actors and actresses on the historical stage. Small wonder then, that Europeans, and in particular, Victorian gender stereotypes were imputed to those not of European origin. Gender discrimination cut across class lines as well as racial lines, but were compounded by these latter considerations. In addition, efforts to christianize indigenous, non-white bonded peoples served to transmit and perpetuate the gender role stereotypes: in the first instance many of the missionaries were female. Wives of missionaries, too, served as educators of prospective converts. Even while stressing spiritual equality in the sight of God, they were careful to preach respect and obedience for those in authority: planters, masters, husbands and men in general over women. Missionary activity, therefore, tended to reproduce the ideal of female domesticity imported from home.

Some of the common casualties in the process of christianizing included all that Europeans perceived as indicative of barbarism and heathenism: polygamous practices or rather concubinage in the case of peoples of African origin, slaves, ex-slaves; *suttee* or widow burning in the case of peoples of Indian origin: indentured immigrant labourers and time-expired resident Indian labourers.

European overlords patted themselves on the backs when these practices were stopped, and proceeded to replace them by their own, more civilised and christianised forms of gender exploitation and gender role stereotypes. They mistakenly perceived the inferior status of indigenous women as being the logical outcome of backward cultural traditions and the absence of christianity, rather than see it for what it was, i.e. part of the world-wide system of gender oppression, a system made concrete by their own stereotyping and by the effects of their own imperialistic interaction with those they considered "lower races". Colonial peoples, male and female alike, were all seen, as Strobel says, as 'children of lesser gods', an inferior order of being on the scale of creation.

Enslaved women in the Caribbean were expected, therefore, to exhibit the stereotypical female characteristics like all other women but at the same time, to work as hard as or even harder than the men, to feel the lash of the whip like the men, to bear children and watch them sold from their breasts into slavery and not feel pains of separation which the naturally emotional, passionate sex, designed for maternity and for nurturing, ought to feel. In fact, they were expected, despite their hardships and heartaches to keep productivity at the accustomed levels. The furore was quite notable when the 'ameliorationists' proposed to abolish flogging of female slaves. Planters objected vociferously, on the grounds that the female slaves were the most intractable, the most insubordinate, the most prone to give offence. They certainly did not fit the ideal of an easily manipulable property, and therefore care should be taken in attempting to elevate them over their male counterparts, as over their white sisters in Europe, who were still subject to flogging in factories before the passage of the Factory Acts (1832–47). It would be a grave mistake, they cautioned, to try 'to legislate the blossoms of spring into autumnal fruit'. In fact, it was of utmost importance for the planter class to maintain control over the female slave population, particularly with the abolition of the slave trade, for their pro-natalist strategies could only be effective within the atmosphere of control from above. Lucille Mathurin Mair, Marietta Morissey, Barbara Bush, Hilary Beckles, Bridget Brereton and others who write of the experiences of female slaves point out that not only did the female slaves refuse to be slotted into pre-defined European gender role categories such as the one which saw women as 'instinctive child-bearers' but that, as the planters' complaints indicate, slave women were always resisters. They took part in revolts, they joined and often led the Maroon groups and found every imaginable way to subvert and undermine the slave system and frustrate the planters' attempts at effective social control. In fact, to understand fully the slave woman's experience of resistance, we need to delimit the boundaries between accommodation and resistance somewhat. It was easier for the men to organise and participate in revolt and rebellion than for the women, but the experience of oppression and sexual exploitation made the horrors of slavery a more real, day to day terror for the women, and therefore, it was of utmost importance for them to find all sorts of means, overt and covert, to undermine the system. Slave women could not sit patiently by awaiting the chance to revolt or runaway, which may only come in the 'sweet by and by' while facing exploitation on a daily basis in the 'bitter here and now'. They therefore turned more readily to what has been viewed as 'strategies for survival' or 'accommodationist tactics': feigning illness, prolonging lactation, seeking to lower chances of conception, for instance, indicate a long tradition of Caribbean female resistance to enforced gender role stereotypes as to the fact of enslavement. They resisted not merely slavery but also the 'slavery of sex', thus heightening the tensions and conflicts within the system and contributing in no small way to its eventual collapse.

From these early times, therefore, Caribbean women established a tradition of defying and resisting European exploitation and stereotyping. We see, therefore, a chronological continuum from pre-conquest time through slavery and the period of Indian indentureship, the post-emancipation era, the development of the peasantry and of creole society into the twentieth century. Female Indian indentured labourers and later free peasants and wage workers worked on the estates at tasks as onerous as those allocated to the men, but worked for less pay. Like the slaves, the Indian women proved that physical strength or lack of it did not necessarily place a woman in an inferior position in the world of actual labour. Field labour was common to male and female alike both during slavery and indentureship. Traditionally, however, as so ably illustrated by V.S. Naipaul in his *House for Mr. Biswas,* female subordination and subservience was the norm among the East Indians, but this was a structure imposed by religious belief and practice, Eastern rather than Western religious beliefs and practices. The European master class was not content with the status quo and sought to invalidate the traditional forms of gender oppression and replace it with Western ones. Resistance came from the entire Indian population, male and female alike. Indian women opted for sticking with the known rather than exploring the realms of the unknown. However, as Bridget Brereton observes in her study of late 19th century Trinidad society, 'traditionally the Indian husband was expected to keep his wife in subjection; this was almost impossible in the plantation situation where women earned their own living and were greatly in demand'. Given the imbalance in sex and class, 'the shame of failure', she continues, 'was wiped out by the cleansing violence of self-righteousness'. Thus the alarming rate of 'Coolie wife murders' was an indication, no doubt, that Indian women were beginning to throw off the restrictions which constrained them. The process was a slow and painful one but an onward and forward one, nevertheless.

The Caribbean woman's active involvement continued apace even after the fact of emancipation. They shied away, like their men, from jobs which reminded them of slavery, preferring to involve themselves in own-account agricultural production, petty trading or to hire themselves in jobs in which they were allowed to maintain some form of pride and dignity. Newspaper advertisements for workers reveal that female ex-slave women were asserting themselves and exercising their rights and independence in choice of occupations.

One advertisement in a Barbadian newspaper dated 5 December 1838 called for a female house servant, 'an honest discreet servant of all work' and cautioned that 'none need apply who are carried away by false and ridiculous notion of freedom and who think it degrading to scour and scrub'. Ex-slave women were demonstrating clearly that they desired to have some control over their own time and labour. Accordingly peasant cultivation proved immeasurably attractive. Others again took work as laundresses, seamstresses, cocoa workers, livestock rearers, tavern keepers, resorting to casual labour on the sugar plantations only as a last resort when cash was needed. Dark-skinned women found themselves debarred from certain occupations, such as domestic service in Jamaica, where, 'coloureds' were expressly asked for.

Like the working class women of Victorian England, these ex-slaves women defied the imposed stereotypes about their role as dutiful wives and about their lack of sexuality. Marriage rates among them were 'scandalously low' and the local newspapers attributed this to 'the general state of unbridled sexual immorality', forgetting that the lavish and astronomical expense of marriage made it a luxury rather than a necessity. The alarming rise in bastardly rates (Brereton indicates that 60% of all births in Trinidad in 1890 were illegitimate) indicates that marriage was not a priority for many Caribbean women, and possibly not an option. 'Single parent families', to use a modern day term, were a norm in late nineteenth century Caribbean society, the family head being invariably the female, thus exploding another Victorian gender myth which the Europeans fought so valiantly to impose on plantation societies. As in working class nineteenth century England, plantation society was a society which threw both sexes together from an early age, where living and working conditions showed little regard for privacy and even less for prudery or female sexual anonymity. Early sexual encounters were a fact of slave life; chastity and celibacy mattered little; female sexuality for the slaves had never been a haloed mystery of zealously guarded virginity. The fallen woman in Victorian society had protested her radically different value system from that by which she was judged. It was not fair to call them 'fallen women', they protested, for they had always been down. Furthermore, they claimed that the middle class was seeing them in a wrong light by claiming that they had 'lost their virtue'. One fallen woman commented: 'I lost — what? not my virtue, for I never had any. That which is commonly, but untruly called virtue, I gave away... I never lost that which I never had... according to my own ideas at the time I only extended my rightful enjoyment.' The same can be applied to the case of the ex-slave Caribbean woman who was expected to suddenly unlearn patterns established over centuries, merely to prove the European stereotypes right and to sweep under the carpet all the unsightly dregs which made life unpalatable for them. But, as the fallen woman had asked, what right had society to have dregs such as they? In their pursuit of sexual liberation and economic independence, the black Caribbean woman in the post-emancipation era stood as a living indictment of the negative impact of plantation society, at least from the European point of view, forever a reminder that they had failed notably to transmit their gender stereotypes wholesale from Europe.

Into the twentieth century, Caribbean women kept up the tradition of resistance to European norms in various forms and fashions. Rhoda Reddock illustrates, for example, the active participation of women in the 1937 Butler Riots. In fact, she notes, of the nine persons arrested and accused of the murder of Charlie King, five were women. And outside of the highly visible few, there were the swell of female supporters who gave the lie to the myth of woman's natural docility and acquiescence. Elsewhere in the Caribbean: St. Vincent, St. Lucia, Grenada, British Guiana, Jamaica, during the labour unrest of the 1930s women were among the strikers, the marchers, the rioters. Contrary to popular European stereotypical expectations, Caribbean women were not merely ornamental fragile objects of male admiration, affection, protection and domination, given to filial obedience, diffidence, fainting spells and restricted by physical constraints. Not even the 'cultured women' lived up to this image, let alone the working class women. The failure of the stereotype to take firm hold led to stigmatizing as in European societies (and elsewhere). Business women, for example, were always portrayed as asexual, either fat and husbandless or very thin and emaciated looking, either way illustrating that these were not the ideal feminine types. The suggestion in 1914 that women be allowed to become members of the Port-of-Spain municipal council provoked a furore of protest in Trinidad society; the newspapers were flooded with letters from 'concerned citizens' all seeking to put women in their place, advising that should this suggestion be acted upon, the Municipal Council meetings would become like 'screaming sessions' in a 'cockatoo house' — utter confusion would take hold. For the sake of all humanity, therefore, letter writers urged that 'good sense' be allowed to prevail, by denying such uncharacteristic and unnatural rights to women.

The above related incident illustrates that while it can be legitimately argued that European gender stereotypes did not apply to Caribbean women and, for the most part, were not internalized by many Caribbean women throughout history, the fact still remains that such stereotypical values were successfully imposed on the culture and on the society at large, making the climb to the pinnacles of liberation and full equality all the more difficult and protracted a process. In many areas of Caribbean life, therefore, the stereotyping persists. In the education system, for instance, gender stereotyping is still evident in the curriculum, as in the process of socialization outside the walls of the schools. From womb to tomb, the sexes are slotted into different niches in life: the 'pink for girls', 'blue for boys'; ideology as is evident, even in the uniforms of a Kindergarten run by the University, which is supposed to reflect the highest levels of enlightenment in any society. Small wonder, then, that by the time girls reach secondary school age, they feel what is believed to be a 'natural inclination' towards the 'softer' subjects and away from technical or vocational education, for example, and from the 'harder' disciplines. Even at the secondary school level, the textbooks reflect the gender stereotypical views held by the larger society, thus serving to reinforce these notions from an early age.

CONCLUSION

The point I would like to make, in the final analysis, is that gender stereotyping has not only put pressure on our women but also on our men, who equally did not conform or fit in to pre-defined European male stereotypes. It is not in keeping with the notion of 'machismo' to do lots of things considered to be rooted within the female domain, like cry, show emotion, tend to babies. The fact of gender stereotyping therefore has put the spotlight back on the Caribbean male. In the twentieth century, and especially since the sixties and seventies, Caribbean women have made considerable strides towards sensitizing themselves about issues which affect and have affected their sex over time. They have formed themselves into organisations and support groups aimed not only at their own consciousness but that of their entire society about the 'Women Question' as it obtains in this region. Accordingly, their achievements thus far are noteworthy. They have been effecting change in concrete ways for all Caribbean women. However, as one of my colleagues put it recently, 'It is now the male who has become the endangered species'. Psychotherapists have documented the significant rise in male clients between the ages of 18–25 claiming impotence or other problems of sexual performance stemming from insecurity and low self-esteem. At the core of the problem is their inability to deal with the new sexually liberated female, and what they perceive as the marginalisation of the male from his accustomed role. The answer does not lie in trying to put the 'Bacchanal Woman' firmly back in her place, but in teaching men to move away from trying to live up to false myths and stereotypical notions of their nature and function. The task now is to look torwards and work towards a new gender consensus, a new equilibrium between the sexes, a new concept of gender relations, which John Stuart Mill defined as 'mutual superiority', a task which can only be accomplished through radical changes in the education system not only in the text books and curriculum but from the levels of policy and in the process of socialization of both sexes from childhood. It may take generations but for our own sakes and the sake of all future Caribbean peoples, we cannot ignore the challenge.

SUGGESTIONS FOR FURTHER READING

Bauer, C. and Ritt, L. (eds.), *Free and Ennobled: Source Readings on the Development of Victorian Feminism* (Pergamon Press, Oxford, 1979).

Beckles, Hilary, *Natural Rebels: A Social History of Enslaved Black Women in Barbados* (Zed Books, London, 1989).

Brereton, Bridget, *Race Relations in Colonial Trinidad* (Cambridge University Press, London, 1979).

Bridenthal, R., Koonz, C. and Stuard S., (eds.), *Becoming Visible. Women in European History* (Houghton and Mifflin, Boston, 1987).

Bush, Barbara, *Slave Women in Caribbean Society 1650–1838* (Heinemann Caribbean, Kingston, 1990).

Mair, Lucille, *The 1986 Elsa Goveia Memorial Lecture: Women Field Workers in Jamaica During Slavery* (Department of History, University of the West Indies, Mona Campus, 1986).

Morissey, Marietta, *Slave Women in the New World: Gender Stratification in the Caribbean* (University of Kansas Press, Lawrence, 1989).

Reddock, Rhoda, 'The Women in Revolt', in Roy Thomas (ed.), *The Trinidad Labour Riots of 1937: Perspectives 50 Years Later* (Extra-Mural Studies Unit, University of the West Indies, St. Augustine Campus, 1987).

Rohlehr, Gordon, *Calypso and Society in Pre-Independence Trinidad* (Gordon Rohlehr, Port of Spain, 1990).

Rowbotham, Sheila, *Hidden From History: Rediscovering Women in History From the Seventeenth Century to the Present* (Random House, New York, 1974).

7

The Caribbean Intellectual and Western Education

GEORGE LAMMING

The starting point of critical elaboration is the consciousness of what one really is, and is knowing 'thyself' as a product of the historical process to date, which has deposited in you an infinity of traces, without leaving an inventory ... therefore it is imperative at the outset to compile such an inventory..."

Antonio Gramsci

The term West and Western, applied to education, which may be interpreted very widely as the transmission of culture; these terms, in our experience, represent power which has resided historically in a minority of men who never considered themselves an organic part of the landscape they controlled. Their own inventory provides a record of enormous crimes. But they owed allegiance to a tradition which had never been severed completely from its own humanity, and therefore such a tradition found itself condemned to the human obligation of offering some moral justification for a totalitarian exercise of authority which was, in practice, immoral. For many centuries after the arrival of Columbus in the Americas, Caribbean society provided various examples of this genocidal contradiction.

Columbus' Journals are among the earliest examples of European travel literature at its most exotic.

I saw so many trees very unlike those of our own country. Many of them have their branches growing in different ways and all around one trunk, and one form or another in a different shape, and so unlike that it is the greatest wonder in the world to see great diversity. I can never tire my eyes looking at such lovely vegetation... The birds and flowers are uncommonly beautiful. I was so delighted with the scene, that I had almost come to the resolution of staying here for the remainder of my days... these countries far surpass all the world in beauty and convenience.

This is the language of the salesman whose exuberance is intended to inspire confidence in those who have funded the enterprise which is the discovery of Gold. The native population share a similar uniqueness with the landscape in the beauty of their communal relations.

> They brought us parrots and balls of cotton and spears and many other things which they exchanged for glass beads. They do not bear arms...

A chorus of other voices follow the Admiral's example.

> They put no value on gold and other precious things. They lack all manner of commerce, neither buying or selling, and rely exclusively on their natural environment for maintenance. They are extremely generous with their possessions.

And as though there were no pause in these reflections on vegetation, mineral resource and men; the Admiral reveals his most urgent intention.

> They would make fine servants. With fifty men we could subjugate them all and make them do what we want.

The fifteenth century is compressed into a moment that reminds us of our own: ...we could subjugate them all and make them do what we want.

Image and stereotype become inseparable in a mode of perception that is regulated to achieve a certain moral justification for acts of conquest that will lead inevitably to a people's doom. Within fifty years of his landing, the native population of the Indies would be reduced to an unrecognisable fragment of its own original numbers. Genocide was the first chapter in the post Columbian history of the Caribbean.

The metropole had found an imperial frontier which fed its imagination with a most attractive reservoir of myths. There arose a costly and dreadful concept that would take root in the European mind: the concept of the Noble Savage, most necessary to the Whiteman's experiment in civilisation, and quite dispensable at the slightest sign of resistance to white conversion.

This myth of the Noble Savage would serve two distinct and complementary functions in the essay by Michael de Montaigne, 'Cannibals':

> Our world has lately discovered another, well peopled, and fruitful as this whereon we live, and yet so raw and childish, that we yet teach it its a,b,c; tis not above 50 years since it knew neither letters, weights, measures, corn, nor vines; it was then quite naked in the mother's lap, and only lived upon what she gave it...I am greatly afraid that we have very much precipitated its declension and ruin by our contagion, and that we have sold it our opinions and our arts at a very dear rate...

The Noble Savage here becomes the barometer by which the metropole can measure the delinquencies of its own civilisation; and its confidence is large enough to let it affirm any scale of ruin without feeling loss of status.

A second function of the myth allows for a theory of cultural relativity. Montaigne continues:

> I find that there is nothing barbarous and savage in this nation, by anything I can gather excepting that everyone gives the title of barbarism to everything that is not in use in his own country; as indeed we have no other level of truth and reason than the example and idea of the opinions and customs of the place wherein we live...This nation are savages, in the same way that we say fruits are wild, which nature produces of herself, and by her own ordinary progress; whereas we ought to call those wild whose natures we have changed by our artifices, and diverted from the common order...

We can't be sure what is the common order, but Montaigne would hardly claim it to be the order in which his own intellect resides. Those who are savage in the same way that fruits are wild risk pollution from any contact with Europe; and a worse fate awaits those who, 'changed by our artifices', will, inevitably, collapse into a truly authentic wildness. This is, I presume, the proper category in which we should place the contemporary intelligentsia of the entire post colonial world.

'Man of two worlds', 'split personality' are among the cliché descriptions which impede free dialogue between Europe and those aliens who have mastered the grammar of European thought and employ it for purposes that are in conflict with Europe's conception of itself as the original and ultimate custodians of all human thought.

This is not an easy mountain to climb, if you are in any mood to go climbing. To be Noble Savage is to become invisible to the other. To be converted savage is to be lost in an intellectual schizophrenia that cannot be redeemed.

They are wiser, perhaps, who followed a human tradition of resistance as the Caribs did, and whom the myth elevated to the ranks of barbarism. Indeed, barbarism became the name of any form of effective physical resistance and the condition which separated militant men and women from that state of grace which was white, human, and in essence, superior to all other forms of animal existence.

The Admiral of the Ocean Sea, was a man who sailed with the absolute conviction that God had destined him to be His divine instrument for spreading the faith; this sailor had hardly set eyes on those noble savages before the thought occured, and most naturally, 'we could subjugate them all and make them do what we want'. Subjugation and servitude became the logical instruments of social intercourse between Europe and all others.

From the day of Columbus' arrival the ideology of racism became the foundation of all Caribbean history which, for the next three centuries, would be decided by force.

In *Buccaneers of America,* John Esquemeling, coming some two hundred years after Columbus, talks the only language that Europe understood:

We know that no peace could ever be established beyond the line, since the first possession of the West Indies by the Spaniards, till the burning of Panama...Until that time the Spanish inhabitants of America being, as it were, in a perpetual war with Europe, certain it is that no coasts nor kingdoms in the world would have been more frequently infested nor alarmed with the invasions of several nations than theirs. Thus from the very beginning of their conquests in America, both English, French, Dutch, Portuguese, Swedes, Danes...and all other nations that navigate the ocean, have frequented the West Indies and filled them with their robberies and assaults.

It is almost impossible to do justice to the unique brutality of thought and feeling which became the European consciousness in its insatiable hunger for gold which by the eighteenth century had transformed sugar into the value of steel and oil in our time.

Joseph Conrad (the novelist), in *Heart of Darkness* comes near to catching that atavistic rage when he encounters them in the Congo in the 1890's:

They were conquerors, and for that you want only brute force – nothing to boast of when you have it, since your strength is just an accident arising from the weakness of others. They grabbed what they could get for the sake of what was to be got. It was just robbery with violence, aggravated murder on a great scale, and men going at it blind – as is very proper for those who tackle a darkness. The conquest of the earth, which mostly means taking it away from those who have a different complexion or slightly flatter noses than ourselves, is not a pretty thing when you look into it too much.

But this enterprise, however barbarous in execution and result, can be redeemed by the recognition and practise of a genuine imperial responsibility. 'What redeems it', Marlowe continues,

is the idea only. An idea at the back of it; not a sentimental pretence but an idea; and an unselfish belief in the idea – something you can set up, and bow down before, and offer a sacrifice to...

Conrad, the Pole, the exile, the eternal foreigner, seeking assimilation into the mainstream of English manners and authority, had no doubt where this idea could be located. He admits to having complex feelings about the Boer war, but he knows whose flag deserves his loyalty:

That they – the Boers – are struggling in good faith for their independence cannot be doubted; but it is also a fact that they have no idea of liberty, which can only be found under the English flag all over the world...

This gift of empire which has denied the status of personhood has a long, resilient tradition in the European consciousness. It had taken place much earlier under the agency of the Admiral Columbus. In the Caribbean, murder and torture and rape which initiated the Spanish legacy of syphillis had soon exterminated a people who had surprised their intruders because they 'put no value on gold and other precious things...lack all manner of commerce..., and are extremely generous with their possessions'.

This was not a pretty thing, as Conrad would say. But the Spanish historian Sepulveda, reviewing these horrors more than three centuries before the 1890's Congo holocaust, had already understood the redeeming power of the idea:

> It does not appear to me contrary to justice that they be taught just and humane ways. These people require by their own nature and in their own interest to be placed under the authority of civilized and virtuous princes and nations, so that they learn from the might, wisdom and law of their conquerors to practise better morals, worthier customs, and a more civilized way of life...

Of course, the moral dilemma is not closed by Sepulveda. For Las Casas, a product of the same tradition, would battle with this view, and argue,

> All peoples of the world are men...all have understanding and volition, all regret and abhor evil...No nation exists today, nor could exist, no matter how barbarous, fierce or depraved its customs may be, which may not be attracted and converted to all political virtues and to all humanity of domestic, political, and rational men.

But this Christian humanist perspective would not break ranks with the divine right of Spanish Church to ensure the evangelisation of the Indians. This ambition, now felt as a moral obligation, to control and govern the noble savages of the tropical world from enormous distance carried immense risk and difficulty; but, according to the English sociologist Benjamin Kidd (1902) it had to be undertaken 'if the civilised world is not to abandon all hope of continuing its economic conquest of the natural resources of the globe.'

The civilizing mission was, therefore, inextricably woven into the dominant material interest which had no room in its vocabulary for the word, 'enough', and pursued its ultimate mission as 'the economic conquest of the natural resources of the globe'.

The Western conception of its role matured into a doctrine of imperial responsibility. The rival powers may argue about their appropriate claims to territory; but there was a settled assumption about their hierarchical relation to those who came under their control.

From 1815 to 1914, according to Harry Magdoff in the *Encyclopedia Britannica,* 1978, 'European direct colonial dominion expanded from 35 per cent of the earth's surface to about 85 per cent of it'; a statistic which illuminates Jean Paul Sartre's contention in his introduction Franz Fanon's *Wretched of the Earth:* 'Not so very long ago, the earth numbered two thousand million inhabitants; five hundred million men, and one thousand five hundred million natives.'

So Sepulveda's blunt assertion in 16th century: 'It does not appear to me contrary to justice that they be taught just humane ways' finds almost an exact echo in the more liberal and rational claim of the liberal Lord Acton two hundred years later: 'Subjection to a people of higher capacity for government is of itself no misfortune; and it is to most countries the condition of their political advancement. A nation can obtain political education only by dependence on another'.

And far to the left of Acton, radical and progressive in his critique of Imperialism, J.A. Hobson in the book of that title yields to the received wisdom of the ages and concedes:

> That all interference on the part of civilised white nations with 'lower races' is not *prima facie* illegitimate...but such interference cannot safely be left to the private enterprise of individual whites. If these principles be admitted, it follows that civilised governments may undertake the political and economic control of lower races – in a word, that the characteristic form of modern imperialism is not under all conditions illegitimate.

The decisive influences shaping this world view were the acquisition of knowledge and power: the triumph of science over religion as a direct revelation of reality; and the superior force of arms.

This heritage of imperial responsibility became a natural ingredient in Euro-America's concept of its destiny. It had settled the issue of slavery without disturbing the ideology of racism which would provide the nation with its most powerful bond of unity. The segregation of the Black presence intensified the menace which they posed, and rescued White America from any severe conflict of class struggle among themselves. If democracy could not take root at home, the idea of it could be propagated abroad. Marlowe's idea is at work with a vengeance in the confessions of President William McKinley to a group of senators in 1898:

> I walked the floor of the White House night after night until midnight; and I am not ashamed to tell you, gentlemen, that I went down on my knees and prayed Almighty God for light and guidance more that one night. And one night it came to me...First, that we should not give the Philippines back to Spain - that would be cowardly and dishonourable; second, that we could not turn them over to France or Germany - that would be bad business and discreditable; third, that we could not leave them to themselves - they were unfit for self-government, and they would soon have anarchy and misrule over there worse than Spain's was; and fourth, that there was nothing left for us to do but to take them all, and to educate the Filipinos and uplift and civilize and Christianize them, and by God's grace do the very best we could by them, as our fellow-men for whom Christ also died. And then I went to bed, and went to sleep and slept soundly...

But when McKinley sleeps soundly, we are aroused by nightmares; for these simple, pentecostal crudities would be refined by more intimidating intellectual argument that would become the decisive influence and the moral justification of United States foreign policy. It is stated with characteristic confidence by Henry Kissinger in an essay, 'Domestic Structure and Foreign Policy':

> The West is deeply committed to the notion that the real world is external to the observer, that knowledge consists of recording and classifying date – the more accurately the better... Cultures which escaped the early impact of Newtonian thinking have retained the essentially pre-Newtonian view that the real world is almost completely internal to the observer...empirical reality has a much different significance for many of the new countries than for the West because, in a certain sense, they never went through the process of discovering it.

The old dichotomy of civilized and uncivilized, Christian Prince and Noble Savage acquires a more palatable and deadly device of neatly carving the world up into those who have retained a pre-Newtonian conception of reality, and those for whom the real world is a construct of systematic thought and scrupulous intellectual order.

It does not, of course, explain how the post-Newtonians could have managed to plunge the continent of their origin into the unprecedented horrors of two world wars this century. But that, you may say, might have been a simple domestic miscalculation gone temporarily wrong.

It is within this context of historical and geo-political reality that a substantial body of literature about the Caribbean, in all its languages, created a script or text of its own with all the contours of race and class stratification that is the most familiar substance of our legacy. It is within this context, with its formidable historical and philosophical monument of knowledge and power, that the Caribbean intellectual was formed, and in whom was deposited an infinity of traces, without leaving an inventory of their own.

The word, intellectual, is an embattled field, evoking attitudes of negation and even ridicule. I would like to identify four senses in which we may use this word and identify the particular categories of person whose activities may define them accordingly.

In the first example an intellectual may be considered to be a person who is primarily concerned with ideas – the origin and history of ideas, the ways in which ideas have influenced and directed social practice.

The philosopher's concern is with the way knowledge is acquired; whether the sense impressions are a reliable guide to any truth about reality; and how should the evidence of observation be interpreted. A complex discourse overlays what is more generally understood as the problematic relation of appearance to reality. They begin with a specialised knowledge of some particular area of human activity, say history or the natural sciences, and then proceed to discover how this particular body of knowledge is related to other areas of human thought. Their purpose is to provide a synoptic view of a whole civilisation. Examples would be professional philosophers like Whitehead or Russell; Marx; or, in history, Arnold Toynbee, W.E.B. Dubois, and in our own region, C.L.R. James.

But what would distinguish them, say James and Dubois, from Toynbee and Whitehead, is not the nature or the range of their interests, but rather the specific function they gave to those interests, the concrete purpose which motivated their study of human society. *Black Jacobins* or Dubois' *Souls of Black Folk* and *Black Reconstruction in America 1860–1880* are initiators of the inventory of a folk whose humanity had not been validated, and whose agency in the transformation of the world and the expansion of the concept of freedom remain seriously contested.

Thus, Carpentier writes on the meaning of the Haitian revolution:

> When we take the great encyclopedia edited by Voltaire, Diderot, Rousseau, in the middle of the 18th century in France, and whose ideas had such an influence over the leaders of our Independence Wars, we find that in this great encyclopedia, the concept of independence has a value which is still purely philosophical. One says independence, yes, independence viv-a-vis the concept of God, vis-a-vis the concept of monarchy, free will, up to which point man's individual freedom reaches, but one does not speak on political independence. On the other hand, what the Blacks of Haiti demanded – those who were the forerunners of all our wars of Independence, was political independence – total emancipation.

There is a second and less rigourous sense in which we may use the term, intellectual. These are people who either as producers or instructors are engaged in work which requires a consistent intellectual activity. These may be artists, in a variety of imaginative expression, or teachers or technocrats or academics. The Caribbean academic, often a specialist of great competence and very limited interests, is not necessarily an intellectual in the first sense since he or she may have little or no interest in the nature of ideas or the correlation which exists between separate disciplines. It is not difficult to find in our ranks a historian or social scientist who has very little knowledge of the imaginative literature or the general cultural history of the region whose past he is reconstructing. And a novelist or poet may be an excellent writer with little or no interest in the philosphical questions raised by those particular forms of expression call the poem or the novel. They may indeed consider it unwise to be distracted by such speculation.

Thirdly, we may use the term, intellectual, in a very generalised sense, to apply to a great variety of people whose tastes and interests favour, and even focus on the products of a certain intellectual activity. That is, people who cultivate a love of music in its variety of forms, or the theatre, or have a passion for the visual arts, or for reading a kind of literature which is intended to cultivate the mind and enliven the sensibility; people who would probably regard the current rash of American television as being very destructive of the critical intelligence (which indeed it may have been intended to be). It is important here to make a clear distinction between American exports the advertising industry insists should be dumped on you, and a certain quality of American television which, at its best, is irresistible as an exercise in popular education and intellectual vitality.

Such people may represent a very wide cross-section of occupations. They overlap with elements in the second example: teachers, technocrats, and academics, and constitute what I shall call the domain or area of mediation. They are of the most critical importance in contributing to the inventory from within and making it available. I shall choose the academic literary critic as one example of a Caribbean intellectual who occupies this domain of mediation.

The context in which we teach and learn is always a decisive influence on the practice and content of what we call knowledge. It may define and even limit our sense of the domain of mediation: that's the areas we locate our activity in, forging vital links between sources of knowledge and the wider consumption of facts. We are speaking of men and women who make their living in the class room. This is at once a great advantage and a serious limitation: to have spent all your working life in school. Some started there as babies; climbed by scholarship and other means to institutions that got higher and higher, almost beyond reach; especially after migration across the ocean to the original citadels of learning.

The Western tradition of imperial tutelage required this initiation, and deposited, among that infinity of traces, the tendency for specialisation; not only within a specific area of intellectual enquiry; but a colonial allegiance to the institutional requirements and the hallowed agenda of the metropolitan institution. The acquired tools of analysis and the vocabulary of critical exposition are among the infinity of traces now woven into a specific mode of perception. There is a certain magic in this metropolitan air that increases its potency on return to native ground.

This Western tradition has always been very selective in its recruits for the consolidation of its mission; and its political control of the native ground created an environment in which Caribbean intellectuals would compete for distinction in worlds where there is a great scarcity of knowledge about the issue they argue about as specialists in the field.

It was and remains a difficult legacy to overcome; a system which had severely restricted the distribution of this form of property which we call knowledge. And knowledge is a form of property. The more difficult it is to acquire, the more prestigious it becomes as a social commodity. Hence the enormous and primitive respect for medical doctors as icons of success. Parallels can of course be found in other areas where the property of knowledge is subject to similar restrictive practices: the historian, the economist; even in medical science where some physicians may get very impatient if you seek to know a little more about the cures they recommend. The domain of mediation is restricted by the mediator's inhibiting sense of his role in expanding the terrain of mediation.

This deformity at the critical level has had negative consequences for writers and those who diagnose what has been written. 'Diagnose' is not an inappropriate word for men and women who insist on calling themselves doctors (it might contribute enormously to the egalitarian character of learning if we got rid of these meaningless emblems). The text is, indeed, spread out like a patient, and after the most meticulous dissection, it becomes etherised. There is a smell of bandages emanating from those accumulated footnotes, a certain odour of morphine lingers over the average thesis. This may be inevitable in a structure where successful careers depend upon the acquisition of such emblems.

So if I may stray from definition of intellectual in the role of academic literary critic to a prescription for such a role, I would propose that the essential and supreme function of the critic/intellectual, in our circumstances, is to be a mediator of text; and the area of mediation must travel beyond the enclave of specialist and student, or specialist in contention with specialist; it must attempt to travel beyond this domain of mediation to link the human substance of the text to the collective consciousness, the continuing social reality which has, in fact, nurtured the imagination of the writers. So the critic/intellectual, in our circumstances (which requires the compiling and preserving of the native inventory) needs also to cultivate the skills of the journalist, the temperament of urgency so common in the evangelist, intervening in public debate over issues which they can easily identify in the literary texts which they mediate.

This role of mediation (as a force of resistance against the Western hegemony) cannot be cultivated where the critic/intellectual functions almost exclusively within an academic enclave where the text offers a battleground for conflicting diagnoses between specialists and their students who may also aspire to the role of 'teacher'. Such enclaves define and limit the terrain of mediation. And it would also be true to say that, in the case of Caribbean literature in English, this enclave offered possibilities for a certan kind of mediation.

It is possible to trace the evolution of Caribbean literature as it graduated from the status of exotic and eccentric report to that of text as a genuine, organic report of experience of a specific social reality (in other words the inventory of an identifiable fold). We passed through and survived a period in which the early novels were simply heard of, without the benefit and challenge of an informed critical response. The broad mass of our population had always been excluded from the culture of book reading. Even where there was critical literacy, and a lively intelligence for dealing with the hazards of survival, the structure of the school had not prepared them for the book as a companion which followed them beyond the school. And the gradual formation of an educated middle class suffered the defects of the context in which they were schooled.

Reflecting the political economy which shaped their values, the book – like other kinds of social commodity – achieved respect only as an imported product. It lost all reality when it appeared as an indigenous creation. Education had made this class a serious obstacle to development, and hostile enemy against any struggle for cultural authenticity, for the compiling of the native inventory.

It was here that the critic/intellectual from within the enclave of specialists, beginning with Mona, struck the first serious and recognised blow on behalf of the literature as an indigenous creation. They had authority to speak for literature in the grand sense of what is known as classics as well as literature in the concrete sense of what was happening on native ground. And their students, who were absolute beginners, got their first baptism in self-recognition through the elucidation of these native texts. The critic/intellectual, in this context helped to elevate the book of the region about the region from neglect and even ridicule to the status of text which required study, investigation, analysis, exposition.

We entered the curriculum. But in this process of sanctification the enclave had bypassed a wider world where the terrain of mediation stopped. It is true that many of these students would become teachers (and very different from their predecessors) serving as messengers of the text. But the message had no continuity beyond the classroom and the moment of graduation. Nevertheless, a small acre of ground had been captured. And that is an important contribution from this category of intellectual.

It is these two categories of intellectual; those who occupy a domain of mediation (academics, technocrats, teachers and the more general enthusiasts of forms of cultural expression) who may restrict or extend the terrain of mediation. They are critical to any viable concept of sovereignty. Sovereignty is not possible where the majority are excluded from this process of the collective control of agendas and continuing self-definition.

The sovereignty of a literature cannot be guaranteed by the excellence of individual works of the imagination, or the ingenuity of discourse between writers and their critics. The sovereignty of a literature depends on the possession of the text by the total society over the most varied terrain of mediation. The text has to become familiar and an ordinary part of daily conversation.

Books stay alive only when they are talked about in a variety of situations by people who recognise that the book is talking about them and may have originated with them. This is all that is meant by the term 'classic' in reference to any national literature. And every literature is a national literature. They do not endure exclusively by virtue of the gifts of the writers; but largely through the persistence of those mediators (intellectuals of categories 2 and 3) who persist in extending the terrain of mediation. It helps to be part of the machinery of a ruling class, as was Thomas Arnold of Rugby who contributed enormously to the number of intellectual casualties we would honour as loyal subjects of that formidable imperial enterprise which we have called Western Education.

But there is a fourth sense in which the word intellectual may be applied to all forms of labour which could not possibly be done without some exercise of the mind. In this sense, the fisherman and the farmer may be regarded as cultural and intellectual workers in their own right.

Social practice has provided them with a considerable body of knowledge and a capacity to make discriminating judgements in their daily work... If we do not regard them as cultural and intellectual workers, it is largely, I think, because of the social stratification which is created by the division of labour, and the legacy of an education system which was designed to reinforce such a division in our modes of perceiving social reality. But the evidence for what I'm saying is there. Woodville Marshall in 'Notes on Peasant Development in the West Indies since 1838' states:

> Peasant activity modified the character of the original Plantation economy and society. The peasants were the innovators in the economic life of the community. Besides producing a greater quality and variety of subsistence food and livestock, they introduced new crops or/and reintroduced old ones. The peasants initiated the conversion of those Plantation territories into modern societies. In a variety of ways they attempted to build local self-generating communities. They founded villages and markets; they built churches and schools; they clamoured for extension of educational facilities, for improvements in communication and markets; they started the local co-operative movement...peasant development was emancipation in action.

This is an achievement of cultural and intellectual activity of the highest order. But you cannot see it that way; because you have been trained to locate such people in an entirely different order of social evaluation.

For the average Caribbean intellectual the domain of mediation does not extend to the class as agents in any mutual exchange between the educated and the untutored. But for Walter Rodney it was precisely here that the act of mediation had to begin. He believed that it was here, in this neglected segment of the civil society, that the most dynamic force of transformation resided. In his *History of the Guyanese Working People* he sought to explode the myth of Indian passivity before the tyrannical constraints of the Plantation; documenting their capacity for strike force; and a variety of ways in which the inter-action of these two peoples were carving out a new ground of social reciprocity.

The arrival of East Indians in the Caribbean, as indentured labour, in the 1830's coincides with the emancipation of slavery and the gradual withdrawal of freed African labour from the European plantations, especially in Trinidad and Guyana. The end of the old slave imposition is the beginning of a new slave arrangement. Indians were subject to the pass laws which tied every man and woman to the particular estate to which each had been assigned. Any violation of this law led to imprisonment with hard labour. Indian workers alternated between the jail and the hospital which was often used as a camp for those who withdrew their labour in protest against conditions of work and the particular role they had been given in the Planter's strategy to curb and erode the radical potential of free African labour.

African free labour lost its power to bargain wherever there was a reservoir of indentured Indian workers. An artificial division was planted within the ranks of labour with consequences which became more complex and debilitating in any struggle against the plantation. The system nurtured a rural working class, occupied mainly in sugar and almost entirely Indian; and an urbanised working class that would be predominantly of African descent. The politics of resistance became obscured or submerged by conflicts of demographic interests, and the more dangerous scenario of cultural antagonism. And each group viewed the other through the filter of that European power which had brought them at different times to the same region for precisely the same purpose.

Rodney wanted to participate in overthrowing the hegemonies of the plantation and its Western institutions; to work towards the emergence of an alternative consciousness. He did not share the view of many of his colleagues that scholarship should seek to achieve a posture of neutrality. (For he knew that McCauley school boys had been taught the definition of an island as 'a piece of land entirely surrounded by the British Navy'.) He believed that history was a way of ordering knowledge which could become an active part of the consciousness of an untutored mass of ordinary people. He did not only argue with those who had taken permanent refuge in the enclave of research and doctoral pursuit. He walked and talked with those African and Indian peasants and workers who had become the *raison d'etre* of his intellectual activities. He had initiated in his personal and professional life a decisive break with the tradition he had been trained to serve; and died in the conviction that the only fruitful emancipation was self-emancipation; that ordinary men and women should be intellectually equipped to liberate themselves from those hostile forms of ownership that are based exclusively on the principle of material self-interest.

We know, to a degree we didn't know some decades ago, that Africans and Indians have a remarkable record of resistance to the same force of domination which sought to appropriate their future, and to define for all time what would be their destiny. But this knowledge is still largely archival; it is locked up in an enclave of scholars and research workers, consultants and technocrats. It is a knowledge which still awaits mass-distribution, and which, therefore has not yet become the shaping influence on the consciousness of those whose recent ancestors had made it possible. It is not inscribed in consciousness.

Given this peculiar history of discontinuity and estrangement within a new landscape of resistance and rebellion against the apartheid control of labour, the victories of organised labour in their struggle to democratise the region; and the continuing struggle, however embattled and confused in its manifestations to set new, post-imperial agendas; and define our reality; these processes over a long time and through much conflict and travail have also evoked a creative response from Cuba to the Guyanas, and produced, in literature both imaginative and polemical, and in all the art, and in religion (as in Haiti), a very distinctive type which is of Caribbean formation, and recognisable as Caribbean in the expression of its cultural and intellectual life. But there is a severe limitation imposed on us by the 'inherent dominant mode' of the Western legacy, which limited the boundaries of intellectual enquiry through the geo-political balkanisation of the region. So whereas English or French intellectuals would choose all Europe, as a singular civilisation and culture for their field of exploration and recovery, the Caribbean intellectual has been fixed in the habit of digging up exclusively the small island enclave whose language zone corresponds to the particular metropole whose institutions have largely fixed his agenda of discourse and made him one of their own.

It is rare to find a Caribbean historian or social scientist who takes the entire region as his field of enquiry and engages in a comparative study of the particularities of each. So Martinique engages in dialogue with itself and Paris, the Hispanic territories responded to a Spanish and wider European orthodoxies; the English speaking Caribbean, ignorant of debate among their neighbours, made their accommodation with an exclusive English tradition, yielding now to a new North American hegemony.

A specific feature of the region is the peculiar origins of our arrival here. The indigenous American Indian peoples trafficked and settled from the Southern mainland as far north as Cuba. Soon these island territories would be without an ancestral host – very different from the mainland, where the American Indians persisted and planted their signature in a decisive way on the cultural evolution of much of what is called Central and Latin America today. This Caribbean became an imperial frontier fought over by every known European power in a struggle to establish what was perhaps their first experiment in capitalism overseas.

The major journeys from Africa and Asia into this archipelago were organised to lay and consolidate the material base of this experiment. This human cargo would have started out in total ignorance of destination. The original experience of African and Asian is the experience of a controlled and violent alienation from the produce of their labour; alienation from the meaning and purpose of human labour. And they were often strangers to each other, even when they had derived from the same continent. It must have required enormous spiritual resource to survive the brutalities of control, the perils and anxieties of the unknown, the suspicion and insecurity which attend all human response in that tentative journey from being stranger, even hostile stranger, to becoming neighbour, friend, and partner in a common struggle of resistance.

So the Caribbean may be defined as the continuum of a journey in space and consciousness; through various stages of crossing from original homeland to island enclave; from enclave to enclave, or the fugitive, erratic pursuit of fortune and meaning within each enclave (migration from rural hideout to urban chaos).

It is or has to become our discovery of the meaning of this severance, the conscious confrontation with the fact of our collective separations from original homes of spirit; the absence of an ancestral hinterland; the balkanisation of all island dialogue to correspond to the orthodoxies of separate metropoles; the political reluctance to transform an elitist social order into an egalitarian encounter of person and person, territory and territory. A profound awareness of the Caribbean nature of our relation to the world, at the material and cultural levels of negotiation, would make each territory more authentically itself than any previous experience could contest.

The major groups of African and Indian descent have been engaged in a continuing struggle against cultural suppression. Each group has been invited at different times, and in different ways, to erase or even scorn its spiritual heritage; and each group at different times has created a force of resistance to this demand. The Indian demand for cultural authenticity is a healthy development; not only for people of Indian descent, but for all societies in the region, since it forces us to deal with our own definition of ourselves, and not through the filter of an external agenda. There is a gulf which now inhibits the Euro-creole element from engaging, free from all racial anxiety, in the intellectual life of the region. But if we consider the examples of Cuba in the 19th century (Marti especially); Hostos and Betances in Puerto Rico; Ortez and Alejo Carpentier and Luis Gonzalez in our own time; or the novels, *Wide Sargasso Sea* by Jean Rhys, Phyllis Alfrey's *Orchid House*, Geoffrey Drayton's *Christopher;* the historical monographs of Karl Watson; we see more than glimpses of the possibilities which await us here.

In Barbados we have talked habitually of the white world as though it were a monolithic, seamless creation, which it is not. It is a world that has retained its peculiar features of social stratification which are obscured by a defensive closing of ranks against the incursions of the black majority. That white voice is still largely silent, except on those occasions, now very frequent, when it is discussing the management of money. It is an important part of the inventory of cultural asset which remains incomplete.

I don't think there has been anything in human history quite like the meeting of Africa, Asia and Europe, in this American archipelago we call the Caribbean. But it is so recent since we assumed responsibility for our own destiny, that the antagonistic weight of the past is felt as an inhibiting menace. And that is the most urgent task and the greatest intellectual challenge: how to control the burden of this history, and incorporate it into our collective sense of the future.

SUGGESTIONS FOR FURTHER READING

Columbus, Christopher, *Journal of First Voyage to America. With an introduction by Van Wyck Brooks* (Books for Libraries Press, Freeport, New York, 1971). Many versions of Columbus' journal have been published; one of the most recent examples is John Cummins, *The Voyage of Christopher Columbus. Columbus' own journal of discovery newly restored and translated* (Weidenfeld and Nicolson, London, 1992).

Conrad, Joseph, *Heart of Darkness and the Secret Sharer; the complete texts* edited by Franklin Walker (Bantam Books, New York, 1968).

Drayton, Richard, and Andiaye (eds.), *Conversations: George Lamming, Essays, Addresses and Interviews, 1953–1990* (Karia Press, London, 1992).

Fanon, Franz, *The Wretched of the Earth* (Penguin, Harmondsworth, 1967).

Hobson, John A., *Imperialism. A Study* (Allen and Unwin, London, 1938 — reprinted 1961).

Marshall, Woodville, 'Notes on Peasant Development in the West Indies Since 1838', in *Social and Economic Studies* Vol. 17, Sept. 1968.

Montaigne, Michael de, 'Cannibals', can be found in *The Essays of Montaigne. Translated by E.J. Trechmann, with an introduction by J.M. Robertson* (Oxford University Press and Humphrey Milford, London, 1935).

Rodney, Walter, *A History of the Guyanese Working People, 1881–1905* (John Hopkins University Press, Baltimore, 1981).

8

The Collapse of the Soviet System: Implications for the Caribbean Left

GEORGE BELLE

Whenever there is a social crisis of quantum leap proportions I believe, philosophy must reassert itself as a source of cognition. Indeed, if we are to have 'understanding', there is no alternative. The German philosopher Hegel said that 'the higher maturity or stage which any Something can reach is that in which it begins to perish'. To that comment C.L.R. James adds, 'It is at this state that subjective reason is compelled, COMPELLED, to intervene'. This lecture will demonstrate how I have come to support these perspectives of James and Hegel and in doing so I will aim to clarify issues arising from the topic before us for discussion.

The Soviet system was partially a consequence of Marxist Thought and analysis. It was also the institutional expression of a social movement. With some qualification the 'Caribbean Left' manifests to a lesser degree both of these aspects of the Soviet system. We need to understand the essence of both of these aspects, if we are to identify or start to identify the implications of the collapse of the Soviet system. This is why we must go to philosophy and there is no path which for me is satisfactory at the present time and circumstance. I am a dialectician; and for me it is in the understanding of dialectics, that the source of cognition can be found in philosophy. Karl Marx was a dialectician; he learnt his dialectics from George Hegel. Lenin was a dialectician; he learnt his dialectics from Karl Marx and Hegel. C.L.R. James was a dialectician, a Trinidadian and a Caribbean man; he learnt his dialectics from Karl Marx, G.W.F. Hegel and V.I. Lenin.

I wish to start this demonstration of a path of cognition by going to James in his *Notes on Dialectics* and through James to Hegel. James quoted Hegel from his *Science of Logic*. There Hegel states:

...the period of fermentation with which a new creation begins seems to be past. At its first appearance such a period generally wears an aspect of fanatical hostility toward the prevalent systematisation of the older principle; it is also, partly, fearful of losing itself in the wilderness of particulars, while it shuns the labour required for scientific development, and in its need of such a development grasps, at first, at an empty formalism. The demand for the digestion and development of the material now becomes so much the more pressing. This is a period in the development of an age, as in the development of an individual, when the chief business is to acquire and maintain the principle in its undeveloped intensity. But the higher requirement is that the principle should be elaborated into systematised knowledge.

And James continues with Hegel where he states: 'But it is the nature of the content and that alone which lives and stirs in philosophic cognition, while it is the very reflection of the content, which itself originates and determines the nature of philosophy'. James says that what Hegel has said here tells us what '...is the key to the Hegelian dialectic and therefore to marxist (sic) thinking'. The significance of this however, he argues, is the recognition that thought '...is not an instrument you apply to a content...content moves, develops, changes and creates new categories of thought and gives them direction'.

For example in the case of the labour movement, our social movement, James says, 'Labour acts empirically and then its innumerable acts crystallize in a formed movement, an organization, a category'. One such category for example is a revolutionary international. Once that takes place says James 'a new development has been added to thought'.

However, once such categories have been developed, it is an error of thought to continue to think in one set of forms, ideas, categories; when in fact content has moved on. That is to say content having moved on, has laid the basis for development of thought – extension of thought – new thought. James speaks of 'revolutionary international', and 'reformist international'; these are categories he says, which 'are "finite, fixed, concrete clear', because we can know what they mean. But then he asks: Do we indeed know what they mean? For they are categories based on specific content. So he concludes 'it is from conforming to finite categories in thought and action that all deception originates'. All deception originates from conforming to finite categories.

James' point is that we must recognize that categories move. But Hegel asserts that in the process of cognition 'understanding makes determinations and maintains them'.

To illustrate this Hegel analyses the philosophic concepts of *Understanding* and *Reason*. Hegel says there are three broad divisions of cognition:
1. Simple, everyday, common sense, vulgar empiricism, ordinary perception.
2. Understanding.

3. Dialectic.

Understanding for Hegel in philosophic terms is 'thinking in finite categories'. When there is recognition that categories move; and you know how and why they move; then your method is that of *Reason* and the tool to comprehend reason is the *Dialectic*.

It is the view of these two dialecticians that two different philosophic ends are achieved by *Understanding* and *Reason*. Hegel says 'Understanding or knowledge by means of the categories is...incapable of knowing the *Things in Themselves*'. That is to say Understanding does not allow perception of absolute reality. Nor does common sense or empiricism, pure and solely, facilitate perception of that thing-in-itself, the absolute. The absolute is the creation of Reason – you speculate and create truth – so Reason is 'speculative truth', in Hegel's phrase. The *Absolute*, the 'things-in-themselves' – the things as they really and comprehensively are (i.e. absolute reality), is the creation of reason – or 'speculative truth'.

Now those comments there by James and Hegel have a great deal of Plato and a great deal of Pharonic Egypt in them. Now what does Pharaoh have to do with the collapse of the Soviet Union? I say Pharonic Egypt has relevance for both aspects we started with, both method and social movement; but we will come back to that later.

We are immediately dealing with 'things-in-themselves' and 'speculative truth', and Hegel defines it thus:

> Speculative truth, it may also be noted, means very much the same as what, in special connection with religious experience and doctrines used to be called Mysticism. The term Mysticism is at present used as a rule, to designate what is mysterious and incomprehensible: and in proportion as their general culture and way of thinking vary, the epithet is applied by one class to denote the real and the true by another to name everything connected with superstition and deception. On which we first of all remark that there is mystery in the mystical, only however for the understanding which is ruled by the principle of abstract identity; whereas the mystical as synonymous with the speculative, is the concrete unity of those propositions, which understanding only accepts in their separation and opposition. And if those who recognize Mysticism as the highest truth are content to leave it in its original utter mystery, their conduct only proves that for them too, as well as for their antagonists, thinking means abstract identification, and that in their opinion, therefore, truth can only be won by renouncing thought or as it is frequently expressed, by leaving the reason captive. But, as we have seen, the abstract thinking of understanding is so far from being either ultimate or stable, that it shows a perpetual tendency to work its own dissolution and swing round into its opposite. Reasonableness, on the contrary, just consists in embracing within itself these opposites as unsubstantial elements. Thus the reason-world may be equally styled mystical, not however because thought cannot both reach and comprehend it, but merely because it lies beyond the compass of understanding.

So Hegel says, there is mystery in the 'mystical', in 'speculative truth', only however for 'understanding'. So what is the difficulty with 'understanding' besides its making of determinations finite? It is that understanding is none-the-less a necessary stage of cognition. James says 'until you fix things in thought in their precise limited finite form...you cannot move a step. You can't begin to discuss'. This is so because understanding is a form of negation. James argues 'understanding' does not take objects as common sense or label them, just as they are. It categorizes them, puts them in order: 'It negates their immediate common sense aspect'. Because its categories assume a permanence however, the very contribution of understanding to cognition, i.e. its transcending of vulgar empiricism and common sense, leaves it open to attack from this lower aspect of cognition. 'Understanding' should have moved immediately on to 'Reason', to 'speculative truth': but it stays with its ossified categories and common sense seems to rule O.K.

Hegel states in the *Logic*:

> It is by referring to this opposition of understanding to sensation or feeling that we must explain the frequent attacks made upon thought for being hard and narrow, and for leading, if consistently developed, to ruinous and pernicious results. The answer to these charges in so far as they are warranted by their facts is that they do not touch thinking in general, certainly not the thinking of Reason, but only the exercise of Understanding.

Understanding opens itself to this because it does not proceed to Reason, i.e. understanding does not begin immediately negating the determinations it has made. James is clear; if you do not move on from understanding to reason, speculative truth, there will be as Hegel says 'ruinous and pernicious results', the ossified categories of understanding will turn into their opposites, because content keeps moving. So in summary we get from Hegel the view that understanding negates the ordinary data of sense, 'analytical thought' and creates the determinations of understanding i.e. creates categories, universals. James says, it creates them and sticks to them.

But Reason negates that determination of understanding as soon as it is created and proceeds to create a more adequate universal, ad infinitum. In James' words, 'There your get the distinction in Reason which on the one hand negates the determinations of Understanding and at the same time creates a higher truth by speculation'. This is Hegel's concept of 'Mind'. 'Reason' in its negative and positive aspects, for James, is 'the great force for negation and creation is continuous'. Philosophic cognition then is not the study of philosophy per se; it is cognition of any object; and we have identified here dialectical cognition.

Let us take another step towards confronting further the issue before us. We are concerned, the people who asked me to talk here are concerned, with the implications of the collapse of the Soviet system. So the questions in the philosophical context of my examination must be: (a) what was the

Soviet system? And (b) What has collapsed? We can seek to answer these questions and get some answers at the philosophical level for the time being, and do so in the context of our philosophical emphasis.

Hegel has said in respect of social history that a philosophy is fully developed in its details and applications only when its main principles have come to be taken for granted and to that extent have become retarded in their speculative development.

In respect to this comment, what did the Soviet Union represent? There are many conclusions from various schools of thought, even (and for me most importantly) within the Marxist movement and Marxist thought itself. The 1977 constitution of the Soviet Union described the U.S.S.R. as a socialist society, building communism i.e. it was socialist, not communist, but building communism.

Mikhail Gorbachev by 1987 was saying: No! The U.S.S.R. is still constructing and still has to construct socialism, because of the distortions of Stalinism. Leon Trotsky and his Fourth International usually argued that the U.S.S.R. was a case of bureaucratic distorted socialism, the consequence of the dull headedness of Stalin and his epigones. C.L.R. James said it was state capitalism, but the necessary determinant stage of development of the labour movement, in its struggle for socialism and against capital and it will be negated. The West, the Bourgeoisie, essentially described it as a communist totalitarian system. The 'Caribbean Left' perspective on the U.S.S.R. ranged from an almost unquestioning support to downright suspicion. The U.S.S.R. was a socialist system model for some, to others embarrassing political baggage. We should remember that many of the leaders of the Marxist and other left forces in the Caribbean matured politically out of the civil rights, black-power New-Left era of the late 1960's to early 1970's. Those who therefore supported the Soviet Union unquestionably did so in many cases having overcome an ingrained suspicion of that system. Others who supported did so more critically because of a developed black consciousness and nationalism. Still others were never comfortable with the Soviet Union because of a 'race first' point of reference. Many of the 'Caribbean Left' including the Marxists, contributed to the New-Left critique of soviet communism, which must be seen as one of the ideological branches of critique which influenced the maturing, years later, of the *perestroika, glasnost* movement in the U.S.S.R. and the Eastern bloc.

In my view, however, it is more important for us to return to some of the original critique of the U.S.S.R., such as the Stalin-Trotsky controversy over 'Socialism in One Country'. This thesis of Stalin's was in fact the end consequence of a debate and power struggle between at least three factions of the Bolshevik party's leadership after Lenin's death. There was on the one hand Nickolai Bukharin's advocacy of socialist construction which took account of Russia's backwardness and with a sensitivity to the need for a genuine socio-political partnership between the proletariat and the massive

Russian peasantry. There was Leon Trotsky on the other urging permanent revolution and rapid industrialization even at the expense of a peasantry-proletarian alliance. And there was Stalin, party bureaucrat and organizer, watching his rivals de-legitimize each other; and waiting. Stalin exhausted all contenders for the leadership and his victory led to unapologetic 'socialism in one country'. It led to what Trotsky contended was an inexorable march to socialist distortion and failure.

Trotsky's theory of 'Permanent Revolution', which he argued on the basis of its grounding in the theory of Marx and Lenin, was posited as follows. Trotsky said:

> The permanent revolution, in the sense which Marx attached to the conception, means a revolution, which makes no compromise with any form of class rule, which does not stop at the democratic stage, which goes over to the socialist measures and to war against the reaction from without, that is a revolution whose every next stage is anchored in the preceding one and which can only end in the complete liquidation of all class society.

Russia, Trotsky contended could not sustain such a process alone: 'In an isolated proletarian dictatorship the internal and external contradictions grow inevitably, together with the growing successes. Remaining isolated the proletarian state must finally become a victim of these contradictions'.

Stalin contended the direct reverse. Russia was a special case with exceptional resources; socialism could be built in one country. C.L.R. James considered that Trotsky took Stalin's theory too seriously. Stalin and Stalinism represented the necessary determinant stage reached by the labour movement in a struggle with international capital. James argues dialectically from the basis of the Hegelian concept of the fixed, ossified, finite, categories of 'Understanding'. Stalinism he says 'has found the objective basis for the fixed categories of Leninism...it operates on a material basis. The games it played with Trotsky over socialism in a single country were the concretization, the stabilising of its ideology. For Stalinism this was a real ideology'.

James is saying Stalinism represented a stage of understanding in the labour movement which did not go over to reason. It did not negate its categories of understanding, it abandoned dialectic in order to justify and preserve itself. This is why I say Stalin, in the proffering and instituting of socialism in one country, effectively 'metaphysically negated' dialectical negation. Trotsky was right in predicting the Hegelian conclusion that the result would be 'ruinous and pernicious'. But James says he was wrong in assuming that Stalin could do what he, Trotsky, wished him to do, or even that what he Trotsky wished was either possible or desirable. For in Stalinism the labour movement had reached a determinant stage. But it inevitably would be negated. James, I think, was right. James realized that this was the basis for a whole range of workers and revolutionaries having to 'accept' Stalinism or further having to work with the Soviet Union as it was. And this carried forward the struggle against capital of course, with costs, and, of course, with non-acceptance in many or most cases of Stalin's morality or immorality. But can we gainsay the impact of that Stalinist state on international events, especially in the colonial world, which included the Caribbean? Its impact (even with Stalin) on the struggle against capital. This is why the Gorbachevian critique of Stalin also carried features of Trotsky's critique in it and perhaps so could not be successful in the particular sense of dialectical negation, although it has understandably laid a basis for dialectical negation in a general but essential sense in my view. We will come back to that later.

Stalin therefore brought Marxism and the social movement, socialism, to a condition where they were 'retarded in their speculative development', this was an imposition consequent on his ossification of categories. The main principles of socialism had not in fact come to be taken for granted. Almost everyone agrees on this one, on the evidence of what was produced at the theoretical level under Stalin; and we know that the Soviet model is responsible for a fixed, rigid, ossified view of socialism, which plagued or is an encumbrance for many Marxists, and for almost all non-Marxist socialists.

Thus, at a time of retarded speculative development main principles were not taken for granted. Rather there was a fear by Stalinism 'of losing itself in the wilderness of particulars'. This happened when there was so much space, so much further to go in terms of 'speculative truth'. How else do we explain the lively Marxist analysis outside of the Soviet bloc, inclusive of the Caribbean? And how do we explain at a far earlier stage in the movement, the rich controversy within Marxist analysis provided by the work of a James himself or a Rosa Luxembourg?

Let us look at Luxembourg, her contribution on organization, her controversy with Lenin. This is important too. Important because it concerns the party, the vanguard party, the Leninist vanguard party. This institution and theory of organization is very central to Marxism-Leninism and very central to the Soviet Union and almost all Soviet institutions, and it became a model of organization of revolutionary Marxism internationally, inclusive of the Caribbean. But let us be clear; Lenin (as James argues), as a thorough going dialectician, came to his organizational concept because he wished to overcome specific backwardness in the Russian labour movement, a backwardness he perceived in comparing it with the German movement. In this way Lenin felt he could move the Russian labour movement forward in a way critical to making the Russian revolution.

Lenin negated the category of the Menshevik labour party in order to construct the Bolshevik party. So what Lenin did was dialectical. In that sense we really miss the central contribution and example of Lenin when we ossify his category, make it a fetish, and fail to appreciate that it was his mastery of dialectical negation that preserves Lenin's outstanding historical role in and contribution to the labour movement. This is why I do not agree with the view that the crisis of the Soviet Union was a crisis of Leninism. It is also why I maintain, it was a crisis of Stalinism, which had in fact negated Leninism but ossified Lenin's categories. For Leninism should be appreciated according to why he introduced the vanguard: not in the vanguard in itself.

But the determination that was the Soviet Union and the determination that is the vanguard party and the 'understanding' which it thus represented was a part, seemingly a necessary part or stage of development, of the movement. That is what Hegel meant when he said: 'it is also fearful of losing itself in the wilderness of particulars, while it shuns the labour required for scientific development and in its need for such development grasps, at first, at an empty formalism.' Nevertheless what we are doing now is looking at Luxembourg for an insight into the potential of 'speculative truth', in so far as she raised questions about the adequacy of Lenin's Russian category. She fully appreciated Lenin's needs and his context of struggle. But she was most aware of the possibility of a Stalin and was aware of what ossification of a category would mean for the labour movement. She sums up their concern in the following comment:

> ...Social Democracy is not bound up with the organization of the working classes; rather it is the very movement of the working class. Social Democratic Centralism must, therefore, be of essentially other coin than the Blanquist. It can be nothing but the imperative summation of the will of the enlightened and fighting vanguard of the working class as opposed to its individual groups and members. This is, so to speak, a 'self-centralism' of the leading stratum of the proletariat; it is the rule of the majority within its own organization.

Lenin did not have the means to get to where Luxembourg was at. I have no doubt that he understood it. But he also understood Russia. And there was the opening for Stalin. If Stalin wished to advance Lenin (post-seizure of state-power) there is where he would have gone. He would have continued on until he had negated Lenin's Bolshevik vanguard. But Stalin, to accomplish 'socialism in one country', 'metaphysically negated' (i.e. negated in a non-dialectical way) the Bolshevik party. Stalin accomplished this through a mechanical transformation, via purge and execution. By such means Stalin removed two-thirds of the leadership of Lenin's party in order to consolidate Stalinism. To that extent he had 'negated' the Bolshevik vanguard, but not by dialectical negation, which might have taken him to Luxembourg. Instead, the consequence of Stalin's deed led to a result, both 'ruinous and pernicious'.

Luxembourg felt that Lenin's party of the 'best of the best' was '...not at all positive and creative, but essentially sterile and domineering. Lenin's concern' she says 'is essentially the control of the activity of the party and not its fruition, the narrowing and not the development, the harassment and not the unification of the movement'.

I believe that Lenin was more dialectical than is suggested there. And certainly his intentions and motivation were more about overcoming Russian backwardness and so to overthrow Tsardom and construct socialism. But

Stalin's early succession to leadership, after Lenin's untimely early death and Stalin's subsequent ossification of the determinations of Lenin, achieved Luxembourg's prediction. C.L.R. James however has a most revealing conclusion based on Lenin's determination, and Stalin's ossification of understanding; but we shall get to that later.

What is interesting is that Mikhail Gorbachev, although seeking negation of Stalinism, also pursued this end undialectically. Gorbachev in fact repeated Stalin's metaphysical negation of Leninism minus the blood and physical liquidation practiced by Stalin. For Gorbachev had by 1991 removed almost, if not entirely the leadership of the Communist Party of the Soviet Union which had been in place at the time of his accession of the post of General Secretary. To that extent he had 'metaphysically negated' Stalin's legacy, as reformed all the same by Kruschev and Brezhnev. He was caught in the 'particular' more fatally, in a political sense, than Stalin. Where Stalin consolidated his rule, Gorbachev unsuspectingly undermined his. In the process, in my view he failed to accomplish the only possibility of dialectical negation, which was to strengthen socialism via the Soviet 'determination'. Of course, this was something which James would say was inconceivable anyway.

But this is what Gorbachev claimed he intended by his initiation of *perestroika*. Here personal ambition derailed by the greater "political maturity of the labour movement" as James would have said, brought him to grief and the Soviet Union with him. Gorbachev was guilty of "ideological electicism...lack of theoretical clarity...hypertrophic ambition...endless thoughtless reorganisations" as a former Soviet ambassador to Poland stated at a central committee plenum in 1990. Thus Gorbachev's *perestroika* became a farce.

Perhaps an overconfidence in the 'understanding', or a lack of clarity in its character, led Gorbachev (as propaganda certainly would have induced one to) to the conclusion that the accomplishments of socialism meant its principles had been taken for granted. Moreover *perestroika, glasnost,* the new-thinking, were proffered as necessary to the U.S.S.R. and so as necessary to the world. This was a 'socialism in the one country' assumption, again a Stalinist assumption. Gorbachev acted out his origins.

Marx himself had said of course in the opening of his *18th Brumaire of Louis Bonaparte* that: 'Hegel remarks somewhere that all facts and personages of great importance in world history occur as it were twice. He forgot to add...' Marx said '...the first time as tragedy the second as farce'. It fits Gorbachev either as a second Lenin or as a second Stalin.

Hegel also commented on the role of the individual in social history, a comment which might address the positive effort of Gorbachev. In the context of what Hegel perceived as 'the spiral of history', he says: 'the cunning reason...sets the passions to work for itself, while that which develops its existence through such impulsion pays the penalty and suffers loss...the particular is for the most part of too trifling value as compared with the general: individuals are sacrificed and abandoned.' This feature is repeated constantly throughout history, hardly on a grander scale than with the tragic hero Gorbachev. In his *Corporate Power in Barbados: The Mutual Affair* Hilary Beckles writes: 'My grasp of history...has shown...that those persons who initiate the struggle are frequently brushed aside by those who came through the back door, appeal to the oppressors, and are given assistance in their rise to positions of power.'

Now let us use this illustration to open the door to discussion at another level. Where are we at? Hilary was trying to make capitalism work for the people; otherwise he says there is going to be crisis. I said in 1987 right here at the Steel Shed that a study of Barbadian history revealed that within ten years, in just about ten years a crisis was due here in Barbados. Barbados' history promised crisis and insurrection for this country ten years hence. The crisis now building in this country and which we all are living through is not a Sandiford* crisis. It is a crisis of international capital and a crisis of all the petit bourgeois bureaucratic class.

The Soviet Union has fallen, 'Socialism' and 'Communism' are dead; but capitalism is in no less deep crisis with the collapse of its supposed nemesis. Let us connect these aspects: capitalism, the fall of the Soviet Union, the Caribbean and the 'left'. Remember, James said Stalinism was a determinant, a stage of understanding, even a necessary stage; but it was ossified and will be negated. Negated to what? You want to know, where we are going? You want to know what to do? We can follow James. James says:

> Dialectical logic is the science of tracing by what laws in what way, notions, our concept of things, change, to know that they change, to know how they change constantly to examine these changes. Scientific method is the examination of an object in its changes, and the examination of our concepts of that object, watching how both change, doing it consciously, clearly, with knowledge and understanding.

James says that this logic and method guided him in his search to find 'essence'. That was Hegel's search and this is what Marx and Lenin learnt from Hegel: the definition of essence, the essence of a thing or a being. What they found was that 'essence' is 'a movement of negation'. That is why Luxembourg had said social democracy is not the organization of the working classes, it is the very movement of the working class. And this is Hegel's definition:

> Becoming in Essence – its reflective movement — is hence the movement from Nothing to Nothing and through Nothing back to itself. The transition or Becoming transcends itself in its transition: that other which arises in the course of this transition is not the Notbeing of Being, but the Nothing of a Nothing – which constitutes Being – Being exists only as the movement of Nothing to Nothing and thus is Essence; and Essence does not contain

* Mr. E.L. Sandiford is current Prime Minister of Barbados.

this movement in itself but is this movement, an absolute show and pure negativity, which has nothing without it that could negate it, but negates only its own negativity, which is only in this negation.

Dust to dust! Ashes to ashes! So 'Being' exists only as the movement of 'Nothing' to 'Nothing'. The issue is not that essence contains this movement. It does not contain this movement: it is this movement.

What we are, each of us, is a movement of negation. Our essence, our being is a movement of nothing, continuously. This is how we have our being, and how the experience of our being is stored up. 'Determination' assists this stage but does not persist, and this is how our essence represents, as well, process and development. By being a movement of negation essence can become anything and movement continues nothing to nothing, with essence negating its own negativity and consequently achieving, in between negations, 'being' – at a point fixed by 'determination'. The essence is the fact that something continually becomes something else and negates it, because it is not what the thing that is becoming wants to be. Essence is therefore a movement of stored up being as well.

We can illustrate the significance of this discussion for what we are about. For this mode of cognition used by James made him state that even though Stalinism represents ossified determination and in his view was pernicious and ruinous, it was, in the context of the struggle between labour and capital, a necessary stage of development. But the relevance of the discussion is also related to the basis of the transcending of that stage of 'being' of the labour movement. It is also very important to the cognition of the nature of the negation which is to come. And James assured us that negation would come. And we have today the collapse of the Soviet Union and Soviet system.

Let us look at some of James' conclusions, reached some forty years ago, as he extrapolated by means of this logic and method. Speaking to the question of organization, speaking on what Lenin intended by his theory of the party, in the struggle against Tsardom and in the movement to achieve socialist revolution, socialism, James says: 'What was vanguardism in Lenin's day is now an essential part of the whole population. The other of Menshevism was Leninism. The other of Stalinism is an international socialist economic order, embracing from the start whole continents'. There are shades here of the New World Order and, further, of Immanuel Wallerstein's World-System theory. James says further 'the truth can only be where it makes itself, its own result'. The proletariat itself will smash Stalinism to pieces. This experience will teach it its final lesson, that the future lies in itself, and not in anything which claims to represent it or direct it'. James reached this position after quoting Hegel as follows:

In the course of its process the Idea creates that illusion, by setting an antithesis to confront it; and its action consists in getting rid of the illusion which it has created. Only out of this error does the truth arise. In this fact lies the reconciliation with error and with finitude. Error or other-being, when superseded, is still a necessary dynamic element of truth: for truth can only be where it makes itself its own result.

'...error...superseded is...a necessary dynamic element of truth.'

For James, Hegel, like Luxembourg would have rejected the party, as teacher of the masses' 'free creative activity'. The proletariat would have instead, to overcome bureaucracy and manipulation, consequent upon the party. There is an implication here applicable to all bureaucratic organization. We shall see the significance of this more clearly when reference is made later to Alvin Toffler's views on this matter.

But there is a special place here for the conscious organization that arises in special relation to spontaneity, within revolutionary politics. i.e. Stalinist politics and bureaucracy and James says:

> ...free creative activity can only come into existence when it is faced with something that only free activity and free activity alone can overcome. That is the point of transition to a higher existence...The Stalinist bureaucracies thus become a stage of development. Free creative activity becomes immeasurably more concrete in our heads. Our notion of Socialism changes...

James' conclusions go further: 'Organization as we have known it has served its purpose...The task is to abolish organization'.
And further: 'The task is to call for, to teach, to illustrate to develop spontaneity'.
And further: 'The new organization, the new organism will begin with spontaneity i.e. free creative activity as its necessity'.
Further: 'Free activity means not only the end of the communist parties. It means the end of capitalism'.
Alvin Toffler has been producing work over the past two decades aimed at identifying a picture of the future. It is quite dialectical; the new world is growing directly out of the old and it is not George Bush's new world order. In his book *The Third Wave* a sequel to the earlier work *Future Shock*, Toffler states:

> A new civilisation is emerging in our lives, and blind men everywhere are trying to suppress it. This new civilisation brings with it new family styles; changed ways of working, loving, and living; a new economy; new political conflicts; and beyond all this an altered consciousness as well. Pieces of this new civilisation exist today. Millions are already altering their lives to the rhythms of tomorrow. Others, terrified of the future, are engaged in a desperate, futile flight into the past and are trying to restore the dying world that gave them birth...Humanity faces a quantum leap forward. It faces the deepest social upheaval and creative restructuring of all time. Without clearly recognising it, we are engaged in building a remarkable new civilisation from the ground up. This is the meaning of the Third Wave.

Toffler argues that we are living in the time of the death of industrialism and a new social system is arising. He suggests that all the organisations which grew up as reflections and servants of industrialism will die with it and these range across both ideological camps that have divided the twentieth century world, both of which he sees as products of industrialism.

I want us to observe more concretely what James was seeing and what Hegel knew; and what the politics of the present and the future will have to understand: Build and Work within new categories of understanding. I can only give a brief illustration of Toffler, but the implications are very large. He writes:

> The fact is that building a new civilisation on the wreckage of the old involves the design of new, more appropriate political structures in many nations at once. This is a painful yet necessary project that is mind-staggering in scope and will no doubt take decades to complete...In all likelihood it will require a protracted battle to radically overhaul – or even scrap – the United States Congress, the Central Committees and Politburos of the communist industrial states, the House of Commons and the House of Lords, the French Chamber of Deputies, the Bundestag, the Diet, the giant ministries and entrenched civil services of many nations, the constitutions and court systems – in short much of the unwieldly and increasingly unworkable apparatus of supposedly representative governments...All these structures will have to be fundamentally altered not because they are inherently evil...but because they are increasingly unworkable – no longer fitted to the needs of a radically changed world...This task will involve multimillions of people. If this radical overhaul is rigidly resisted it may well trigger bloodshed. How peaceful the process turns out to be will depend on many factors therefore – on how flexible or intransigent the existing elites prove to be, on whether the change is accelerated by economic collapse on whether or not external threats and military interventions occur. Clearly the risks are great...Yet the risks of not overhauling our political institutions are even greater, and the sooner we begin the safer we all will be.

Immanuel Wallerstein writing over a similar period has struggled to have acceptance of his world-economy thesis. We have seen with our own eyes the risk today indisputably of a global system of world capitalism. Soviet socialism has collapsed and Islam is 'under manners'. Wallerstein says this world-economy has been there for 500 years. Buttressing this system as presently formulated are economic integration movements on a continental scale. In these all the same, lie in my view, one of the contradictions of the new world order. Let us remember James' 'Other of Stalinism'; 'the other of Stalinism is an international socialist economic order, embracing from the start whole continents'. How else could we get there but maybe through this present historical farce of a new world order, with its regional integration movements led by the European Economic Community, the I.M.F. and the World Bank? But Wallerstein says:

the concept 'world-economy', assumes that there exists an 'economy' wherever (and if but only if) there is an ongoing extensive and relatively complete social division of labour within an integrated set of production processes which relate to each other through a 'market' which has been 'instituted' or 'created in some complex way. Using such a concept, the world-economy is not new in the twentieth century nor is it a coming together of 'national economies' none of the latter constituting complete divisions of labour. Rather a world-economy, capitalist in form, has been in existence in at least part of the globe since the sixteenth century. Today, the entire globe is operating within the framework of this singular social division of labour we are calling the capitalist world-economy.

Within this thesis which we cannot illustrate at length, Wallerstein recognised 'anti-systemic movements' and it is this which must interest us in the context of our discussion. How does he get there?

To describe this world-economy as capitalist is to assert that it is a single social division of labour based on the integration of complementary production processes, and that the institutions of this world-economy are structured in such a way that they reward more often than not those whose activities are predicated upon the endless accumulation of capital. Over time, the operations of such a system tend to result in the formal rationalisation of the extraction of surplus-value, and to the extent that rationalisation is achieved, it eliminates structures which counteract a polarization of the class structure...A moment's reflection reveals that the formal rationalisation of the system undermines its substantive rationality and thus in the long run its political viability. It is therefore the success of capitalism as a world-system (and not its difficulties) that will being about its demise.

This is why I suspect that the current ideology of free enterprise and democracy, (remember James' free creative activity as necessity), will play the same historical role for capitalism, as the 'blood and iron' monarchs of feudal Europe played in the overthrow of feudal powers. They overthrew the power of their own class, by their alliance with the rising bourgeoisie of Europe, to be in turn negated by that national bourgeoisie. So 'free capitalism', 'bourgeois democracy' as farcical as 'king and country', turns into its opposite, James' 'new organism' with 'free creative activity as its necessity'.

Anti-systemic movements have plagued capitalism in its century of greatest strength, the twentieth century. Wallerstein says that 'Although the U.S.S.R. was not as strong either economically or militarily as anyone pretended, it was just strong enough to create world-systemic space for various anti-systemic forces'. The anti-systemic movement followed national capitalism within a reality of world capitalism. Wallerstein argues: 'The question is whether we shall arrive at a socialist world order by cumulating a series of revolutionary victories state by state until somehow a majority of post-revolutionary states...tips us over some global balance. I simply do not believe this...'

In 1992 we know that that 'determination' of most of the twentieth century has now collapsed or at least entered into profound crisis. So we can understand Wallerstein's point. He concludes:

> I have argued that the state is not the framework within which social action occurs but merely one of the institutions created to sustain and promote the interests of various actors in the real social arena, the capitalist world-economy. It follows that any transformation of capitalism can only be a transformation of this whole. The acquisition of state power by anyone else is an instrument with which to maneuver in the political arena of the World-economy. It is not the only such instrument. It may not always be the most important instrument. And like all instruments it is only useful when placed within a continuing, global strategy...We must take active account of the growing multiplicity of the forms of anti-systemic movements. Scylla is to assume that only one form, a party form, is legitimate. Charybdis is that everything goes. In between we must recognize that the combined and uneven development of the world capitalist system has led and will continue to lead to a combined and uneven development of anti-systemic movements, and that a world struggle involves necessarily serious transnational movements...When the ruling classes have ceased to be self-confident, and are therefore trying to survive in new ways (even in the guise of a transformed world) the acquisition of state power is far from enough to destroy them.

There is much here in my opinion for the 'Caribbean Left' to reflect upon and contemplate; from Hegel to Marx, from Lenin to James to Toffler and to Wallerstein. But consciousness of the oppression of African peoples, racial oppression of black people is also a part of the dynamic of consciousness of the 'Caribbean Left'. George Padmore, Marxist and PanAfricanist; James, Marxist and PanAfricanist. Why? Answer: Necessity. There is no truth without it. I said I would reach Pharaoh again. The 'new world order' threatens the 'third world', the black world, with what Ali Mazrui calls global apartheid. I would add that it even threatens the "third world" with Lebensraum. For now, latently but with great potentiality, there is the possibility of re-assertion of the Lebensraum world view of Nazi Germany.

I am in agreement with the great African and Senegalese intellectual colossus; Cheikh Anta Diop, that 'The history of Black Africa will remain suspended in air, and cannot be written correctly until African historians dare to connect it with the history of Egypt.'

Karl Marx has noted in his critique of Political Economy, and Hegel is said to have often insisted, that the 'end is contained in the beginning'; 'but we can only see the beginning fully as we approach the end'. I referred to Pharaoh when I referred to Plato. I referred to Plato when Hegel defined 'speculative truth'. I know that Hegel was influenced by Plato; and Plato it may surprise you, was an Egyptophile. He lived in 'awe and admiration' of ancient Pharonic Egypt. As Diop says ancient Pharonic Egypt was a negro civilisation and I stress with Diop the description 'Negro', without apology.

We have understanding of that term; it is clearer than 'black'.

I believe that when we look across millennia at what Europe has done to black civilisation, but particularly what it did in the last five centuries, a process of struggle between civilizations can be identified. A struggle starting essentially 2500 years ago represents a definite decline of black global power, a period of 2500 years of envy and revenge by the white European World and, initially, by the Eurasian hordes against the glory of Egypt. This was a period and process essentially of European anti-thesis. It ought to be a part of the destiny of the 'negro left' to resolve this contradiction.

Diop described ancient Egyptian cosmology as 'archaic materialism'. He so described it because of its mix of the mystical with materialism, i.e. idealist materialism. Egyptian cosmology was seemingly dialectical in its construction. One concept of the great pyramid represents it as a material symbol of the mystical sexual intercourse of the gods. James in his *Notes on Dialectics* says that, 'If it is possible to say of Marxism that it is the most idealistic of materialisms, it is equally true of Hegel's dialectic, that it the most materialistic of idealisms'.

I believe that Plato in his borrowing from Egypt, borrowed his concept of the philosopher-king in *The Republic,* from the actuality of the Egyptian God-King, the Pharaoh. The philosopher-king of Plato, combined political greatness and political wisdom in one.

I believe mankind will solve many of the social problems in the twenty-first century if the 'black left' can in a fashion repeat Marx one step on. Where, while Marx said he had turned Hegel right side up by replacing 'world-spirit' with forces of production, so too the 'black left' must turn Plato the philosopher of Europe on his head. By extension Pharaoh would be turned on his head and 'political greatness and wisdom' would thence forth be among the people. James 'free creative activity as necessity' would have come to pass. Egypt's cosmological negation, an Aristotelian responsibility and determination would have been negated.

SUGGESTIONS FOR FURTHER READING

Belle, George A.V., 'Collapse of the Soviet Union: What it means', *Sunday Sun,* 5 Jan. 1992.

Cornford, F.M.,*The Republic of Plato* (Oxford University Press, Oxford, 1961).

Diop, Cheikh Anta, *The African Origin of Civilization* (Lawrence Hill, U.K., 1974).

Gorbachev, M., *Perestroika New Thinking For Our Country and the World* (Collins, London, 1987).

Hegel, G.W.F., *The Science of Logic* (Macmillan, London, 1951).

———. *The Logic of Hegel,* (Clarendon Press, Oxford, 1931).

———. The Phenomenology of Mind, (MacMillan, London, 1949).

Howard, Dick, *Selected Writings of Rosa Luxembourg*, (Monthly Review Press, New York, 1971).

James, C.L.R., *Notes on Dialectics*.

_____. *Hegel-Marx-Lenin*, (Allison and Busby Ltd., London, 1980).

James, George G.M., *Stolen Legacy*, (G.G.M. James, 1954, Asa. G. Hilliard, 1988).

Lenin, V.I , *"What is to be done?"* in *Essential Works of Lenin*, (Bantam Books Inc, New York, 1966).

Marx, Karl, *"The Eighteenth Brumaire of Louis Bonaparte*, in Marx and Engels - Selected Works, vol. 1, (Moscow 1962).

Toffler, Alvin, *The Third Wave*, (Pan Books Ltd., London, 1981).

Trotsky, Leon, *The Revolution Betrayed*, (New York, 1963).

Wallerstein, Immanuel, *The Politics of the World - Economy*, (Cambridge University Press, Cambridge 1984).

9

Europe 1992:
Implications for the Caribbean

PAT THOMPSON*

Dr. Hilary Beckles, the Head of UWI's Department of History at Cave Hill, in his letter to me inviting me to give this lecture said that he was leaving it up to me to specify the concerns which the title of the lecture, "1992 and the Caribbean" suggested to my own mind.

I am grateful to Dr. Beckles for this latitude for several reasons. First, as I believe is well-known, I am not myself a historian and will therefore not be dwelling on such aspects of the 500th anniversary of the arrival of Columbus in the region, as have already been adequately covered in earlier lectures in the series, including a very interesting one by Dr. Beckles himself. In this regard, I will confine myself to a few observations, more as background to the substance of my presentation this evening, than as serious, in-depth analyses.

First, you will note that I referred to the arrival of Columbus in this region and not, as we still tend to hear today, to his discovery of this region. No serious person today disputes the well-organized way of life of our Amerindian ancestors in this region, long before Columbus came here. Nor should they wish to dispute the studied assault on the Amerindians and their life style which Columbus' arrival triggered, amounting virtually to genocide. Little wonder that Carib Chief Irvince Auguste of Dominica sees little to celebrate about, in observing the Quincentennial of Columbus' arrival in this region.

It is, I suggest, also beyond serious dispute that the process which Columbus' arrival and in particular the set of values and attitudes which he brought with him from fifteenth century Europe put in train, led inexorably over

* I would like to emphasize that I am speaking tonight in a purely personal capacity. I do not wish any of the views which I will express or the causes which I will espouse to be ascribed either to the private sector organization whose Chief Executive I happen to be or to any of the Directors or staff of that Association.

time, given the prevailing philosophies of the day, to the practices first of slavery, then of indentured labour and on to the exploitations and grave excesses of colonialism and the colonial period.

The dramatic and fateful encounter of European civilization with our own, starting in the fifteenth century and leading through the major political, economic, demographic and social changes to which that encounter gave rise, have resulted in a wide-ranging and often malign legacy, the effects of which remain with us to this day. Our parlous political condition, our enduring state of economic marginalization, the tensions and contradictions, ethnic, religious and ideological, which continue to characterize the state of our social relations – all of these have their origin in process initiated by the arrival of Columbus and set in motion by the set of beliefs, values and attitudes which he brought from the dominant European environment and culture of his day.

All of that is, I suggest, beyond basic dispute. Where I perhaps differ somewhat from some of my fellow West Indian commentators, in assessing that historical process and the multi-faceted heritage which it has bequeathed to us, is in two respects. Firstly, I insist on seeing the series of major processes and events triggered by Columbus' arrival in their true historical perspective. The world is not a static place. Values, beliefs, attitudes, social systems – all change over time. While the past is invariably a good source of explanation of much of our present, it is not necessarily an accurate determinant of our future. Secondly, in being properly concerned with an assessment and necessary understanding of the injustices, inequities, exploitations and repressions of the past – and we are right in resisting attempts to cover up or whitewash that unsavory record – we should take care not to fall into the opposite trap of an obsessive preoccupation with that past. We must not allow such a preoccupation to blind us to changing conditions and circumstances, to revised beliefs and altered values on the part of some of the former colonizers and exploiters or their descendants, to the extent that we neglect, in our own interest, to formulate new strategies based on current realities. Those realities have the potential to help usher us into a future significantly better than either our severely disadvantaged past or our tenuously surviving present.

It should be noted that some of the ongoing negative aspects of the legacy of Columbus' arrival in our region, persist not only in the Caribbean, but also in today's so-called 'developed' New World of the United States of America. One obvious example of this is the continuing black-white economic and social tensions of present-day America, a phenomenon which in Barbados you seem determined to emulate, although in rather different circumstances. Perhaps the best, current exposition of that specific American phenomenon is to be found in a recently published book by a distinguished, white political scientist in the U.S., Andrew Hacker, entitled: *Two Nations: Black and White, Separate, Hostile, Unequal.* In it, Hacker argues, as a recent 'Editor's Choice' summary in the *New York Times* Book Review of 15 March 1992 put it, that 'unto this day, black people have not received a fair shake as American citizens – and that most white Americans don't believe this.'

This is one – an important one, of Columbus' unhappy legacies to us in this hemisphere: the black-white tensions and inequities of the USA on the one hand and of Barbados on the other. However, if we look at other countries in the English-speaking Caribbean – at, for example, Guyana or Trinidad and Tobago – we shall see different varieties of this specific malign virus which Columbus' arrival bequeathed to us: there is an underlying Black-Indian tension in those societies, with many adverse political, economic and social consequences. But, as I shall argue, I do not believe, in any of the instances I have cited, inside or outside of the region, that we are doomed to live with the baleful consequences of this particular virus. It will definitely not be easy to overcome its disruptive effects and consequences. But I believe that if we correctly analyze the origins of our widespread ethnic problem and its unhappy consequences if left untreated, we can begin to develop effective antidotes to the virus.

We need to develop the wisdom to attend to the deep-rooted underlying causes, as opposed to the cosmetic symptoms and the courage to persist in the face of emotive and highly partisan objections, which seek easy sanctuary in the solidarity of colour, caste or religious affiliation. Education holds the key. If we are able to marshall our educational resources and to deploy them effectively in our Caribbean societies, we can eventually overcome the ethnic factors and begin to create a society qualitatively different from the one which Columbus initiated and his successors bequeathed to us. I believe that we owe it to ourselves as West Indians to develop that wisdom and to summon up that courage which are the essential qualities needed to render the virus harmless and with which an adequately funded and properly organized educational system can furnish us. Towards the end of this lecture, I will have a few further words to say about this important aspect of our overall theme.

In developing my substantive subject of '1992 and the Caribbean' I wish to focus on four main sub-themes. First, I would like to look briefly at the forces which I believe are currently driving the process of integration in the European Community and to point to some aspects of these forces which are changing, as well as to the shifting European and international environment in which the changes are taking place and to suggest that because of these new factors that the precise outcome of the present initiatives in Europe are less clear-cut than is generally assumed. Secondly, I would like to look at our own response – such as it is – in the English-speaking Caribbean – to those seminal changes which are afoot in Europe and to place our regional response in a context which makes it an integral part of an overall response to a larger challenge. That larger challenge is, I believe, rooted in the process of political and economic liberalization which is, in my view, now a dominant feature of the current international relations scene. Thirdly, I would like to examine briefly the current condition of the concept of the 'Third World', with which we have – at least up to the recent past – proudly identified ourselves as members. Does that notion of Third World still mean anything today? Does it have a viable future and if so, of what kind and deriving from which specific factors? Fourthly, and finally, arising from a consideration of the issues raised by the first three sub-themes, I would like, no doubt ill-advisedly, to adumbrate the outlines of a strategy which we in the English-speaking Caribbean should at least begin to examine – if only to arrive at a better one – by way of a response to the certain challenges and possible opportunities with which the events of 1992, in the world, as well as in Europe, will start to confront us.

I am concerned with our future as West Indians: that we should consciously set broad targets for that future, rooted in our own values and cultural norms; that we should devise, implement and monitor wide-ranging strategies, in an attempt to secure that future; that we should, while learning from our past and enduring much of our present, not cease for a moment to believe in ourselves or our potential and in our capacity to influence and to better that future.

Let us, then, look at our first sub-theme: the process of integration in the European Community which has led from the start of serious work on the Single Market with the White Paper of June 1985, through the Single European Act of 1986 to the European Single Market that is to start its formal, legal life at the beginning of next year (1993). Let us look briefly at some aspects of that process and at what lessons those might hold for us in the English-speaking Caribbean.

The first thing to notice is that the integration process, if it is to have substantive results, is a long-distance race rather than a sprint or, to put it in more authentic West Indian terms, a full series of five-day cricket Test Matches, rather than a limited number of 50-over one day matches. Strategy and tactics will both be different in the one, as compared with the other. The idea of a common market or a custom union in Europe was being canvassed as early as in the nineteenth century. Anthony Hartley, a contributing editor to *The National Interest* magazine (published quarterly in the USA by National Affairs Inc.), in an interesting piece in the Winter 1991/92 issue, entitled 'The Once and Future Europe', traces the history of various plans for political and economic integration in Europe. He makes the interesting point that all of those earlier plans arose out of attempts to solve the problems inherent in the relationship between France and Germany. After the Second World War, the advent of the Cold War in Europe between the then USSR and its East European allies on the one hand and Western Europe and its ally, the United States, on the other, was a potent factor in helping France to mainain some kind of countervailing balance against the re-emerging economic might of West Germany.

With the Cold War now effectively over and Germany now reunited, the previous Franco-German balance of power has been altered and a reunited Germany now seems destined to be once again the dominant economic force in Europe. The full consequences of these developments on the process of European integration are still to be felt. Hartley puts it like this, in the piece I have referred to:

> The last two or three years represent a major turning point in European history. After the successive plans for European unity, which have been elaborated throughout practically the whole of the twentieth century, events have suddenly redefined the Europe that is to be united and the nature of its unity. The odds now are that this will take the form of a looser and wider confederation of states whose immediate historic role will be to link Eastern and Western Europe and, finally, to bring Russia into that concert of nations. That Germany should be the chief instrument of this transformation and eventually reconciliation is a paradox and an atonement.[1]

The lesson which we in the English-speaking Caribbean might draw from that analysis is that the integration process does not take place in either a political or an economic vacuum. Power relationships between states aspiring to integrate are constantly changing and the nature and extent of that change will influence the integration process itself. In that regard, I draw to the attention of those who wish to notice it, the beginnings of a recovery from a structured adjustment decline of the economy of Trinidad & Tobago, as well as the first stirring in Guyana of a climb-out of the economic black hole into which that country slipped some twenty years ago. If credible elections are held there this year and the pace of economic recovery accelerates, a clear joint policy initiative by these two countries located at the southern end of the present CARICOM configuration, could revive, indeed transform the region's present integration prospects.

Another point to notice about serious integration is that not only does it require decisive political will and a willingness to cede various aspects of national sovereignty. In addition, a lot of the essential trade and investment groundwork is plodding, unglamorous, but necessary stuff. In a book entitled *'Europower: the essential guide to Europe's economic transformation in 1992'* by Nicholas Colchester and David Buchan, Monsieur Jacques Delors, President of the European Commission is quoted as saying of that dull but vital groundwork, 'It is hard to fall in love with a single market.' Colchester and Buchan go on to add:

> And indeed the prospect of a common standard for pressure vessels, so that they may be traded freely between Aberdeen and Athens without exploding, does not set hearts pounding. But that standard is just one of a myriad of barrier-flattening measures flowing from the European Community's 1992 project. Taken together, they will create the largest single pool of free-flowing goods, service, capital and people in the world. Only when you calculate

what might be done with the economic fruits of this single market, only when the political ramifications of creating it are thought through, does palpitation set in.[2]

The moral for us here in the English-speaking Caribbean seems reasonably clear to me. In matters pertaining to regional integration, we must, as indeed in some other contexts, learn to see the wood from the trees. We must not lose sight of wider goals and greater objectives, economic and political, as we occasionally bog down in the minutiae of regulation-framing, the crafting of regional trade and investment compromises and the mechanics of dispute resolution.

I want to close this necessarily brief look at my first sub-theme with two further quotations from the book by Colchester and Buchan, which both make points that I believe have lessons for us in CARICOM. Firstly, this:

> What makes a superpower? Economic strength is the foundation as Britain learnt, America worriedly senses and Russia must regret. The EC's economy now matches America's for size. It is no longer fanciful to talk of the Community as one economic power: the twelve members have turned themselves into more than a free-trade area. They are letting their systems values and standards infect each other and thereby creating political interdependence and 'ever closer union'.[3]

That last phrase 'even closer union' is wording taken from the text of the Single European Act of 1986. They continue:

> The European Community was launched by a political conviction that Europe should not fight another nationalist war. After a heady first twelve years, its momentum flagged. It was re-launched, not by dramatic street demonstrations and historic surrenders of power, but by unleashing a pent up desire for an open market. This bureaucratic coup triggered changes in the EC's constitution, which in turn refreshed its appetite for political union. Is a federal Europe imminent? No: if that means the United States of Europe, where a president can say with a straight face "My fellow Europeans" and not sound phoney. Yes: if that means that twelve countries have attained such sophistication and share so many basic values that they gainfully submit themselves to common laws and some democratic means of making them.[4]

Three comments: – first, note the crucial, under-pinning role of economic strength. While we in CARICOM cannot aspire to any kind of super-power status, other than perhaps in the league of intellect – and a good thing, too, in my view – we ought not to neglect the sustained building of our economic strength, in order to create the leverage for negotiating effectively for the kind of future we have determined we wish to strive for. Second, note that even the most promising of integration movements will sometimes flag and go into temporary disarray. We must not despair too quickly. Rather, we should look at economic inventives which can inspire a mutual resolution to restart the process. And we should remember that economic revival can lead to a reawakening of the need for closer, political co-operation.

Finally, note that the resolution of integration difficulties can be greatly facilitated by the presence and deployment of techniques which have their origin in democratic ways and means. We have an obligation to try to ensure that each member country of the integration movement is steadfastly adhering to transparently democratic norms and practices. Could it be that in CARICOM, over the last two decades or so, we have failed to make greater progress in our integration efforts partly because we have not been as rigorous as we should have been, in observance of democratic norms right across the Community? I leave my audience to ponder on that thought, while I turn now to my second sub-theme.

Secondly, then, against the background of the general progress and prospects of European integration in 1992, how are we in the English-speaking Caribbean faring? To begin with, I believe that we ought to see our response to the advent of the Single Market as part of a wider response which we would anyway be forced into making, given the current process of liberalization, political and economic, which is now a dominant, global trend. That global process is characterized, in its political dimensions, by a strong tendency towards some version of multi-party democracy. The alleged virtues of the one-party state, trumpeted so vigorously by some colleagues of mine in Guyana back in the 1950s and 60s are now seen, with the collapse of the system in the former USSR and the East European countries, to have been largely illusory, as I remember arguing publicly in Georgetown at that time. There are, it is true, still a few notable hold-outs: The People's Republic of China, Cuba, North Korea, perhaps one or two others in the developing world. But by and large the game is up and as those countries which I have mentioned attempt to combine the practice of authoritarian political principles with some modified form or partial market economy, they are likely to discover that this is akin to trying to mix oil and water. Place no bets or at best hedge them, if you intend to wager on the survival or the resurgence of the one party state. Which is not, let me add, the same thing as saying that multi-party democracy as it is currently practised in say the U.S.A or in Western Europe is without serious flaws or to fail to argue that we must not slavishly imitate those frequently prescribed models, without attempting to correct some of their inherent defects or to adapt them to our cultural norms.

In its economic dimensions, the process of global economic liberalization has put the highly-centralized, essentially coercive, mainly state-dominated model of economic development to flight across much of the world and has enthroned instead, essentially market-oriented models, with a heavy premium on individual freedom and personal choice. The so-called magic of the market is the preferred flavour of at least this economic decade and when last I saw him on television, Milton Freidman was smiling the kind of broad, tolerant smile often associated with experts whose theories come under early fire from their peers, but which subsequent events appear to justify and later generations seek to embrace.

I suppose that since I work, by choice, in the private sector – although I have done tours of duty and national service in the public and diplomatic spheres – that you will expect me to say that I think that the magic of the market is a potent economic force to which we should all pay serious attention. So I will say so. But let me add that I think that there is more to economic development and equitable economic growth than is covered by the theory of market oriented economies. There is, for example, in my view, a clear, and important and abiding role for governments as the framers of overall macro-economic policy, in the maintenance of law and order; in the provision of appropriate economic inventives to the private sector and to other sectors in the society; in the maintenance of an economic climate conducive to private sector investment in the efficient production of goods and supply of services, perserving as far as is possible, a level playing field on which genuine competition can work to the benefit of consumers and society alike; and, above all, in the provision by the state of adequate physical and social infra-structure. In the latter case emphasizing educational and health facilities, in the absence of which the private sector will be unable to effectively discharge its productive role and real economic development will be dangerously skewed. So the magic of the market is necessary in all modern economies. But, by itself, it is not sufficient. Our democratically elected leaders still have much important economic work to do for and on behalf of their societies, in the discharge of which responsibilities, the quality of the leadership they are able to provide becomes a key ingredient for success.

So, we in CARICOM have to respond to this process of global liberalization and our response to the European Single Market is an integral part of the larger challenge. How are we doing? Frankly, not terribly well.

It is essential that we begin by putting our own regional house in order, not only because this is a necessary pre-condition for outlining and agreeing a joint strategy vis-a-vis the daunting challenges and potential opportunities which we face, but also as a base, a platform from which we can begin to design a network of alliances with non-CARICOM regional neighbours and with nearby countries in Central and South America which I believe, would be willing to join forces with us in some areas, creating the political muscle and the economic influence needed to negotiate effectively and to leverage desirable gains, in the global market place.

But, as of now, we still have an uncommon market rather than a Common one. It is still riddled, at intra-regional trade and investment levels with licences, various non-tariff barriers and ambiguous rules and regulations which uncommitted observers have been led to believe are designed to stymie the growth of regional trade and the development of intra-regional investment, although both of these trends would tend to impact favourably on our abiding twin scourges of high unemployment and low foreign exchange earnings. In the process, both our standard of living as well as our quality of life are unnecessarily compromised.

We have begun to talk, despite the incomplete Common Market, about a CARICOM Single Market. We have even set a date for its advent – January 1, 1994. Of course, seasoned observers of the current CARICOM Community process and notably of the persisting absence of adequate mechanisms for monitoring the implementation of Community decisions, have long ceased treating such publicly-proclaimed deadlines seriously. If you never arrive at the office on time in the morning, you can hardly expect to be lauded for punctuality!

But external events are, I believe, going to force our otherwise hesitant hands. The evolution of three mega trading and investment blocs in the modern world – one in Europe, one in Asia, one beginning to form in our own hemisphere, of which President Bush's Enterprise for the Americas Initiative is the catalyst and the current NAFTA negotiations between the United States, Canada and Mexico the alarm clock, set to go off this year or next, depending on domestic political developments in the U.S.A. These events will, I believe, force us to re-think our economic strategy and the paradigm of economic development which we have pursued over the last two to three decades.

Essentially, I think we will have to change gears, to shift emphasis. To see the role of government more along the lines I was describing earlier, along with an increased role for the social partners, the private sector and the trade union movement, both as fully-consulted partners in the process of economic planning and such regulation as is needed, as well as, as primary engines in the process of the efficient production of goods and provision of services. While it is a shift in emphasis rather than a total abandonment of previous roles, given our history and our cultural norms, the change will look like a sea-change to many of us, in the public and private sector alike.

In this shifting pattern, the decisions we make about our own CARICOM Single Market and the speed and clarity with which we implement them will, I submit, be crucial determinants of a viable economic future for the region and an indication of the nature of our basic response to the European Single Market and the NAFTA arrangements, symptoms as they are of the process of global liberalization which I have described. A good deal of worthwhile planning and analysis on the CARICOM Single Market has already been done at CARICOM public sector, senior technician level. What remains to be done – and where we have often fallen down in the past – is early and adequate consultation with the social partners and following that, the exercise of clear political will, which would be reflected in prompt macro-economic policy decisions taken in the context of a defined budget, an agreed timetable for implementation and an adequate mechanism for monitoring that implementation and refining the process on the basis of relevant feedback. Given our past track record in the region, this is a tall order. But I do not think that we have a choice. And the alternative, assuming our customary hesitancy and lack of resolute regional action is stark indeed. I have coined a phrase to describe that alternative. It tells us what our future is likely to be if we continue in our present mode. Here is the phrase:– permanent marginalization (economically speaking) and irretrievable irrelevance (in a global, political sense). It is not a fate to be contemplated with equanimity.

Let me turn quickly, to my third sub-theme. A part of our economic philosophy and of our political arrangements in the English-speaking Caribbean – some would say a reflection of our ideological preference – used to be an identification with the so-called Third World, including our membership of the non-aligned movement. I say 'used to be' advisedly, because I hear less and less both of our Third World identity and of our non-aligned membership from more and more of our elected governments. Clearly, times have changed. the collapse of the Cold War between East and West has, as an inevitable side-effect, altered the nature of the relationship between North and South. We would appear to be very much more on our own these days.

In the same issue of *The National Interest* to which I have already referred, there is another article entitled 'The Third World, R.I.P.' by Owen Harries, who is the magazine's editor. It is, for a West Indian, a somewhat depressing piece. Here for your information are two quotations from the piece. First, on the basic premise of the article:– 'The Third World is dying, if not dead. One may still, I suppose, use the term in lower case to designate a rather vague socio-economic category. But in its upper case sense of a militant ideological and political grouping, it is finished'.[5] Second, on the fact that in the post Cold War World, the prospects for developing countries of not only foreign private investment but also of official developmental assistance, is now much bleaker than hitherto:–

> ...the world's main aid giver and source of investment capital is already, and will continue to be, Japan, and the Japanese – strangers to humanitarianism and guilt – are not a soft touch. They put a premium on self-reliance and self-generated strength, both in themselves and in others. Professor Tahashi Inaguchi of the University of Tokyo expresses it this way:– 'Giving grants in too large amounts spoils recipients. If they cannot manage loan repayments by industrializing the economy rapidly and thus generating enough surplus through self-discipline, their self-strengthening will not be achieved'.[6]

And, some of us think that we already have enough problems dealing with the requirements of the I.M.F.!

Harries goes on to say that in his view, the ability of so-called Third World countries to evoke interest and to lever assistance from the developed world in future, will depend on how they handle two factors in which the developed world does have a deep interest. One is the problem of proliferation of weapons – not only nuclear, chemical and biological weapons and of the ballistic missiles used to launch them, but more generally, the spread of conventional arms and the national and regional insecurities which that spread tends to engender. There is not, I fancy, much for us in CARICOM to latch on to there! Harries' second potent factor is migration. As he puts it:– 'The real prospect of large-scale, sustained and uncontrolled migration from third world-countries to the developed, industrialized ones, with all the tension and liability that would entail.'[7]

Here, I believe, we are on more familiar ground. We have only to look, in our own hemisphere, at Cuban and Haitian migration to the United States and indeed at the differing response to those two varieties of migrants in the U.S. – to realize that the developed world must have – and must demonstrate – a genuine concern to promote self-sustained economic growth in the developing world.

And in Europe, in France, we have only to note the rapid political rise of Monsieur Le Pen, to appreciate what a potent and potentially divisive political force the migration issue has been and will probably again become, on that continent. And our own earlier economic migrants to England of the 50s and 60s will remember how much of a political issue Mr. Enoch Powell was able to make of their presence and that of other Commonwealth immigrants, in those years. And while he did not himself gain great political success from his agitation, he did succeed in getting the U.K.'s immigration rules considerably tightened. So, I forecast, will Monsieur Le Pen, vis-a-vis French immigration rules. But if self-sustained growth continues to elude developing countries, including our own, the immigration problem will not disappear, however the formal immigration rules may be altered.

While Harries does not mention them, I think that apart from his two factors there are several others which we need to bear in mind and to use constructively, in our interest, in an indifferent and often hostile world. Here are two to ponder: first, the traffic in narcotics and what assistance we could and should legitimately ask for, in order to cope with the problem of our own CARICOM countries being used, either as production sites or trans-shipment channels, for the marketing of drugs in North America and Europe; and second, global environmental concerns; not simply those which affect us at national level, but those, like the use of fluorohydrocarbons, with their potential for damaging the ozone layer or the presence of chemicals in the atmosphere which can generate acid rain, given shifts in the prevailing winds. Some of these environmental problems do not recognise national boundaries. Developing countries which in their own interest, as well as in the wider international interest, are willing to constructively tackle these difficult problems need and deserve financial help and various forms of technical assistance.

So, the Third World is no longer, in the changed condition of the post Cold War World, what it used to be, as a catalyst for development assistance from East or West. But all is not lost. If we analyze well, if we negotiate skilfully, if we take common positions in a united front, there are still levers we can pull which will help us to cope better with the challenges of current economic development.

This brings me to my fourth and final sub-theme. What, in the face of trends and tendencies we have noted, most of them inimical to our development prospects, might be the outline of an overall CARICOM strategy which could offer some promise of redressing the present unequal balance and of achieving a better and more secure future for our respective countries and for our region?

I submit that the bare-bones outline of such an overarching strategy, drawing on some of the points made earlier in this lecture, should have features like these: first, it is essential, in my view, that we quickly forge bonds of regional economic unity that are closer than they now are – as close as is practicable. The immediate goals should be to complete our unfinished Common Market and then to move on boldly to establishing a CARICOM Single Market. It may be that not all CARICOM countries are ready to move forward together now to that goal. If that be the case, let us say so frankly now, so that the ones who are ready can move forward without bitterness or rancour, leaving the door ajar for others to join later, when the economic conditions and circumstances so dictate. I believe that, as mentioned earlier, a side benefit of this process of deepened economic co-operation will be a heightened awareness of the value of greater political co-operation, not starting with any a priority assumptions, but following the process logically and constructively to see where it takes us. The only requirement is that we maintain basic democratic concepts and practices, suited to our cultural norms.

Second, that initial re-ordering of our regional house will set the stage for devising a regional trade and investment sub-strategy for CARICOM. That sub-strategy will be our general response to the process of global liberalization I have described and specifically to the challenge and opportunities, already upon us, of the advent of the Single European Market and the imminent conclusion of the NAFTA negotiations. An integral part of this sub-strategy will be the fashioning of tactical and other alliances with non CARICOM Caribbean countries and with countries in South and Central America, who are willing to make common cause with us on specific issues or groups of issues.

Third, we should start a structured dialogue in the region, between governments and their social partners in the private sector and the trade union movement and including other groups as well – the university community, women's groups, the youth movement – about the question of a shift in emphasis in the paradigm of economic development which we have been utilizing in the region for the past two or three decades. While that dialogue is in train, we should without necessarily awaiting its outcome and resolution, proceed to emphasize certain functions and refine certain factors. The factors to be emphasized would include productivity, the pursuit of standards of excellence, and the practice of total quality management among others. The functions to be refined could well include the skills of marketing, especially export marketing and market research and greater funding and encouragement of indigenous research and development, in a context which recognizes our need to develop a strong science and technology base. Those emphases and refinements are needed in public as well as private sectors.

Fourth, while recognizing the importance of a market-oriented economy and the value of a profitable private sector, we also should bear in mind the need for an efficient public sector, able to provide an adequate and up-to-date physical and social infrastructure.

Fifth, we need to ensure the authenticity and credibility of our political systems and arrangements. A part of this task will be to deal openly but sensitively with the development of measures which can avoid or contain disruptions to our national and regional life which will result from a failure to heal those ethnic rifts and divisions in our society which we have partly inherited from our history but which we can exacerbate by neglect or indifference.

Sixthly and finally, we have to remember what a proper definition of economic development is and what economic growth is for. The fruits of that growth must be equitably distributed.

Our Caribbean of the future must not simply be a logical but distant derivation of the Columbus model. We must become, we must ourselves create, a different kind of society; one in which efficiency and growth are balanced by caring and compassion. It shall be a society characterized by an incorruptible system of justice and one in which there is a safety net and avenues of assistance for those temporarily dislodged from the mainstream by the forces of competition and the pursuit of efficiency. We have to help such temporary casualties to find their way back to self-sustaining growth. Can we do it? Can we West Indians, looking at our chequered history and our trubulent present, find the will, the wisdom, and the courage and the imagination to work our way to a more secure and constructive future? I believe that we can. In seeking to convince you about this, let me close with a final quotation, this one from a genuine West Indian source.

I was looking, when preparing this lecture, at the publication put out by the CARICOM Secretariat in Guyana but printed here in Barbados called *CARICOM Perspective* – the double issue, numbers 52 and 53, for the period July – December, 1991. And in thumbing through it, I came upon a guest column (pp. 50–52), featuring an excerpt from an address by a representative of one of the co-sponsors of this lecture series, Dr. Hilary Beckles, on the subject 'Columbus and the Contemporary Disposition within the Caribbean'. As with everything Hilary Beckles writes, it is well written. I did not agree with everything he said, but I want to end by quoting a small part of that guest column which is apposite to the question I have just posed about our capability as West Indians. Dr. Beckles is referring to some of the work of distinguished West Indian historians who have preceded him, like the late Dr. Eric Williams and the late C.L.R. James. He refers to James in these terms:

> But most importantly, C.L.R. James developed a concept of creolisation and the statement that West Indian people inspite of that history, now represent perhaps a unique human species, that perhaps Caribbean people are pioneers of the future; that within the Caribbean, a mind set was created, people who are the carriers of European ancestry, African ancestry, Amerindian ancestry, Asian ancestry; that almost every civilization in the world has brought to focus upon the Caribbean to create economic growth, but resulted in a sociological mix which has created this person called the Caribbean person.
>
> The Caribbean person therefore is a futuristic individual not linked to any one civilization, not linked to any one world view but indeed the conjunctural concoction of all these things. He says therefore that we are value-free people, we are a people who are flexible within this world system, we could live anywhere, we can go anywhere. Caribbean people are the perfectly adaptable creatures that emerged and this represents, he argued in the present system, whereby they all become part of what we call the global village, that we perfectly suited to survive the future because of our history.

I want myself to go just a bit further. Because of our history and who we now are, I don't simply want us to survive the future. I want us to help mould it through our own efforts and imagination a little closer to our heart's desire, so that we and our children coming after us, can live in that future with dignity and reasonable comfort, and at peace with our countrymen and women and with the wide world around us.

NOTES/SUGGESTION FOR FURTHER READING

1. Anthony Hartley, 'The Once and Future Europe' in *The National Interest* Winter 1991/92, p. 53.
2. Nicholas Colchester and David Buchan, *Europower: The Essential Guide to Europe's Economic Transformation* (*The Economist* Books, London, 1990), pp. 7–8.
3. ibid., p. 233.
4. ibid., pp. 237–238.
5. Owen Harries, 'The Third World, R.I.P.' *The National Interest* Winter 1991/92, p. 109.
6. Owen Harries, 'The Third World, R.I.P.'.
7. ibid.

Index

ABC Islands, the, 55–56, 57. *See also*
  Aruba; Bonaire; Curaçao
abolition, 38–39, 40–41, 42, 47, 49, 50,
  51, 72
abolitionists, 50
Absolute, the, 96
academic literary critic, the, 86–87
Acton, Lord, 83
Africa, 91
African, the, 9, 30
African, Caribbean and Pacific (ACP)
  Countries, 59, 60
African Presence, the, 5
Africans, 23, 27, 29, 32, 90, 92
Agricultural Revolution, 67
agriculture, 19, 58
Albemarle, Duke of, 33
Alfrey, Phyllis, 92
Allsopp, Richard, 2
American Revolution, 40, 42, 48
American War of Independence, 43, 48,
  49
Americans, 10
Americas, the, 4, 5, 8, 10, 11, 17, 21
Amerindians, 17, 19, 21, 58, 91, 111
'Angel of the House', 65
Anglophone Caribbean. *See* English-
  speaking Caribbean
Anguilla, 54
animals, 17
Anniwatta, 32
Anstey, Roger, 42
Antigua, 28, 33, 54
apartheid, 5
Arawaks, 18. *See also* Tainos
Archer, Pearce, 47
Aristide, Fr. Bertrand, 59

Arnold, Thomas, 88
Aruba, 55, 56, 57, 60
Asia, 91
Asians, 4, 10, 14 n25
asiento, 41
'Associated Statehood', 54
Atkins, Governor, 33, 35
Atlantic, The, 16
Auguiste, Chief Irvince, 111
Aztecs, 15

Bacchanal Lady, 64–65, 76
Barbados, 41, 45, 47, 53, 92
  Columbus' legacies in, 112–113
  crisis in, 103
  Kalinagos and, 20, 26, 32, 34
  runaway slaves from, 29–30
barbarism, 80
Barbuda, 34
batey, 19
Batie, Robert Carlyle, 41
Bay of Pigs, 60
Beckles, Hilary, 72, 103, 111, 123–124
'becoming', 10
Belize, 54
Bequia, 29
Bering Straits, The, 16
Berlin, Isaiah, 8, 14 n21
Bishop, Maurice, 3
black civilisation, 109
black consciousness, 98
Black-Indian tensions, 113
'Black Legend', 21
Boers, 81
Bolsheviks, 100, 101
Bonaire, 55, 56, 57
book, the 87–88

THE CARIBBEAN AND EUROPE

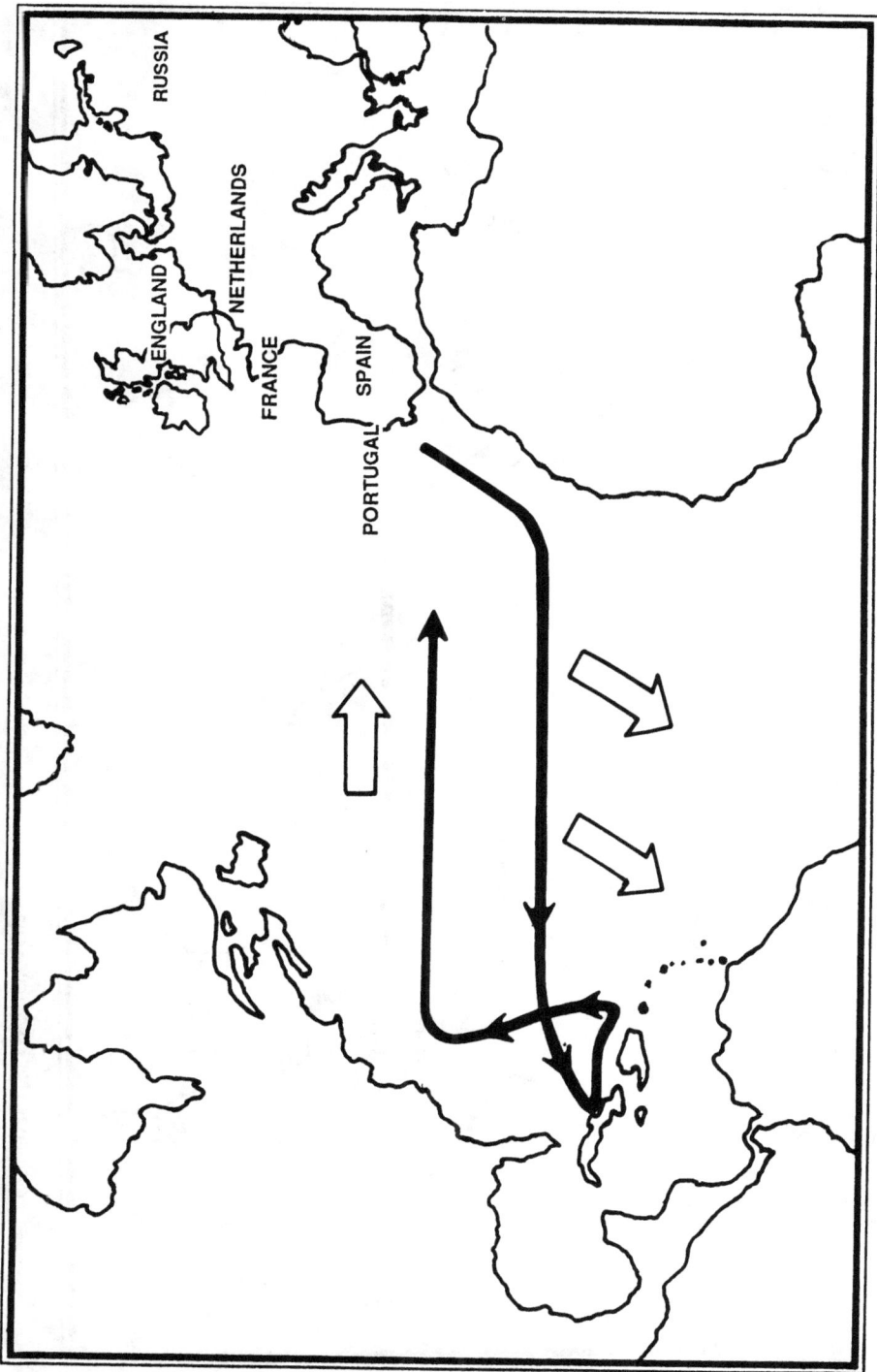

RUSSIA

NETHERLANDS

ENGLAND

FRANCE

PORTUGAL   SPAIN

➡ COLUMBUS' 1ST VOYAGE

⇨ PREVAILING WINDS

THE CARIBBEAN AND EUROPE

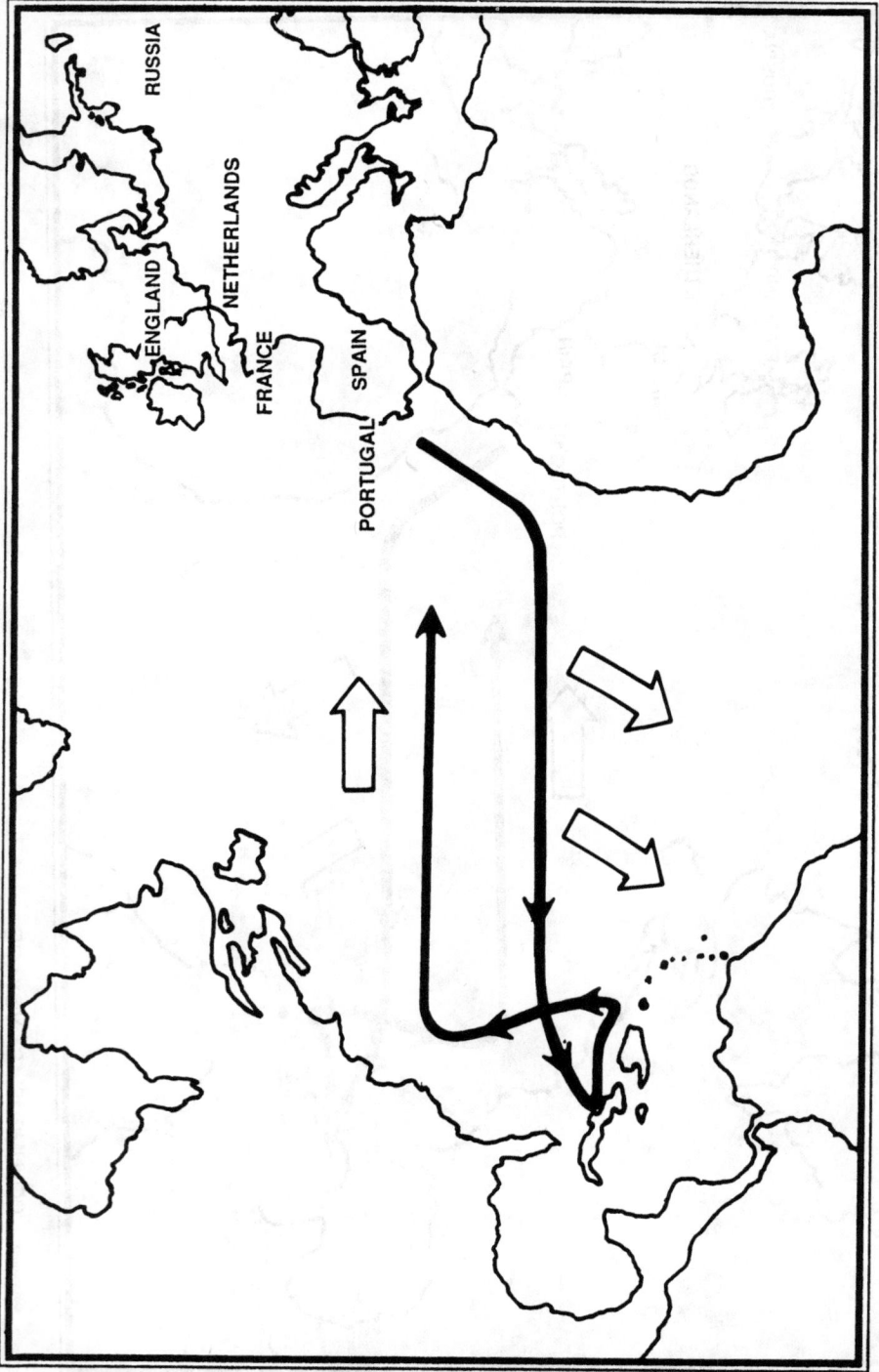

RUSSIA

NETHERLANDS

ENGLAND

FRANCE

PORTUGAL   SPAIN

→ COLUMBUS' 1ST VOYAGE

www.ingramcontent.com/pod-product-compliance
Lightning Source LLC
Chambersburg PA
CBHW061748270326
41928CB00011B/2420